1968

S0-BNH-461

3 0301 00041962 8

VIETNAM
Lotus in a Sea of Fire

Ngọc phân sơn thượng sắc thường nhuân
Liên phát lô trung thấp vị cān

The jade burned on the mountain retains its natural color,
The lotus, blooming in the furnace, does not lose its freshness.

NGO AN (Vietnamese Zen monk,
eleventh century A.D.)

VIETNAM
Lotus in a Sea of Fire

By

THICH NHAT HANH

WITH A FOREWORD BY THOMAS MERTON
AND AN AFTERWORD BY ALFRED HASSLER

LIBRARY
College of St. Francis
JOLIET, ILL.

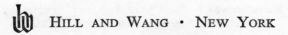 HILL AND WANG · NEW YORK

Copyright © 1967 by Hill and Wang, Inc.
All rights reserved
Library of Congress catalog card number: 67-15652

FIRST EDITION FEBRUARY 1967
SECOND PRINTING MARCH 1967

Manufactured in the United States of America by
The Colonial Press Inc., Clinton, Massachusetts

959.7
N576

CONTENTS

45138

FOREWORD

THICH NHAT HANH is a Vietnamese scholar and a poet, a contemplative monk who has felt himself obliged to take an active part in his country's effort to escape destruction in a vicious power struggle between capitalism and communism. While many of his countrymen are divided and find themselves, through choice or through compulsion, supporting the Saigon government and the Americans, or formally and explicitly committed to communism, Nhat Hanh speaks for the vast majority who know little of politics but who seek to preserve something of Vietnam's traditional identity as an Asian and largely Buddhist culture. Above all, they want to *live* and see an end to a brutal and useless war. He speaks for his people and for a renewed and "engaged" Buddhism that has taken up the challenge of modern and Western civilization in its often disastrous impact upon the East.

This new Buddhism is not immersed in an eternal trance. Nor is it engaged in a fanatical self-glorifying quest for political power. It is not remote and withdrawn from the sufferings of ordinary men and their problems in a world of revolution. It seeks to help them solve these problems. But at the same time it struggles to keep itself independent of massive pressures—whether American or Chinese or Russian—in order to assert certain claims which have never been clearly apprehended or understood in the West. These claims issue from a state of mind which is widespread all through Southeast Asia. To ignore this state of mind is fatal. It must be known and understood.

Thich Nhat Hanh has given us the first really clear and articulate expression of this peculiarly Asian viewpoint. His book is not a piece of inspired agitation but a reasonable, carefully documented and authoritative exposition of historical and cultural evidence. From this book we may perhaps begin to understand why so many fantastic errors and confusions have so far characterized Western adventures in Southeast Asia. Westerners apparently have no idea whatever of the complexity of the social and cultural problems they are wrestling with in Asia. They are evidently entirely out of

contact with the Vietnamese people themselves—dealing almost
entirely with stooges who tell them what they themselves want to
hear. As a result, in order to "destroy communism" they destroy
more non-Communist elements who are working for social reform
and who offer some reasonable hope of an alternative to Communist revolution. This is true not only in Asia but also, and above
all, in Latin America.

A dispassionate and objective reading of these pages will convince any sincere mind that we have too long been clinging to a
comic-strip mythology about Asia. Our political and military activities in Asia are perhaps too often dictated by puerile fantasies.
Fantasies of good guys and bad guys, clean-cut clear-eyed Americans with appropriately subservient Asian friends, and sinister
slant-eyed Asian Communists. Angels and devils, and no one in
between. Anyone who likes us is an angel. The rest are devils.

But in reality, as this book shows, we are confronting the problems of several million very real people whom we have insisted on
treating as if they were invisible because they are nothing like us,
and do not especially want to be like us. We are dealing with a
society and a culture which, because we have no way on earth of
understanding it, we have decided to ignore. These people have
refused to stay invisible, and this culture is demanding respectful
consideration in its unfamiliar, but by no means exotic, complica-
tions. They do not ask us the favor of transforming them into
second-class Americans. They ask us to allow them to be themselves.

Buddhism is much less a matter of organized and institutional
orthodoxy than a *state of mind*. Buddhism does not aim directly
at theological salvation but at a total clarification of consciousness.
It is not so much a way of worshipping as a way of *being*. Exterior
cultural accretions are much less important than they may seem,
and the Buddhist cultural awareness is endowed, as Nhat Hanh
shows, with a mercury-like formlessness which evades the statistical
eye of the Western scholar. The latter peers at Asian social realities
through his refined instruments, and because he does not appre-
hend this elusive consciousness, he thinks there is nothing there
at all. Or else he sees something obscure and frightening which,
purely because it disturbs him, he decides must be "communism."
Thich Nhat Hanh makes it quite clear that he and his Buddhist
associates are by no means Communists. They are struggling with
the problems of communism in a courageously realistic way. And
they are frustrated by the oversimplifications and stupidities with

which we insist on driving them, whether they like it or not, into the arms of China.

The outspoken and shrewdly critical pages which Nhat Hanh devotes to the past history of Catholicism in Vietnam are, let us admit it, very important. Catholic conservatives are probably not going to like these pages. They will perhaps attempt to dismiss them as mere anti-Catholicism and hostile prejudice. I am perfectly prepared to sympathize with the sincere grief of these people, but I regret that I cannot agree with them. Thich Nhat Hanh is not hostile to Catholicism or to the Church. Certainly these pages make a Catholic squirm with embarrassment. They should do so. The Second Vatican Council has clearly admitted that there is no place left for empty triumphalism in the Catholic estimate of missionary history. Serious errors have been made, and they have brought great discredit on the Christian message. These errors were due not to the faith and to the Gospel, but to nationalistic and cultural prejudices, attachment to rigid organizational patterns, or obsession with institutional façades and political prestige.

The Council has implicitly or explicitly admitted such errors, and has declared that they must never be repeated.

This book shows clearly that progressive Catholics in Vietnam are in full agreement with what the author himself says. The pages on Catholicism in Vietnam are severe, but salutary. The mature Catholic conscience cannot afford to ignore them.

Doubtless there is another side to the complex historical question, and scholars can in due time restore the balance, if it needs to be restored. But for the present, it is imperative to recognize that this is what thousands of people in Vietnam actually feel about Christianity. Here we have a forthright statement of their case against it: together with a willing admission that this view is now being radically altered, due to the example of progressive Catholics in Vietnam today. Hence, there is in fact a very real hope of constructive collaboration between Catholics and Buddhists in a peaceful Vietnam—if such a thing ever becomes possible.

Speaking however of "progressive" Catholicism, let us not be naïve. For all his authoritarianism, we must not forget that Ngo Dinh Diem was profoundly influenced by a French Catholic thinker who was far more radical than many progressives are even today: Emmanuel Mounier. This book takes account of Diem's progressive intentions, but shows how they were frustrated by corruption and stupidity. It is not enough to read Leftist magazines and absorb the fashionable ideologies of advanced intellectuals accepted as leaders in France! That is why this book is not proposing a new ideological system, but rather appealing to a respect for common fundamental human values as the only obvious realities upon which we can base sincere efforts for peace and reconstruction. We cannot hope to help men if we do not respect them as human beings and value them in their existential reality.

One of the great tragedies of our time is that in our desperate incapacity to cope with the complexities of our world, we over-simplify every issue and reduce it to a neat ideological formula. Doubtless we have to do something in order to grasp things quickly and effectively. But unfortunately this "quick and effective grasp" too often turns out to be no grasp at all, or only a grasp on a shadow. The ideological formulas for which we are willing to tol-erate and even to provoke the destruction of entire nations may one day reveal themselves to have been the most complete deceptions. Already, in the case of Vietnam, the American conscience is trou-bled by a sense of tragic ambiguity in our professed motives for massive intervention there. Yet in the name of such tenuous and questionable motives we continue to bomb, to burn, and to kill because we think we have no alternative, and because we are re-duced to a despairing trust in the assurances of "experts" in whom we have no real confidence: but who else is there to listen to? Perhaps we can begin with a little homework on a book like this. It teaches us that there are in Asia whole worlds of thought and concern we have not yet dreamed of.

This explosive little book will doubtless upset many American readers. If so, we can only say they need to be upset. We all need to be grateful for the *first clear articulation* of views and claims that we have hitherto completely ignored. These are the views and claims of masses of people whom we do not know, whom we have never tried to understand, in whom we have never really been interested, and whose interests we now believe ourselves uniquely competent to defend with armed power on a massive scale, even at the risk of a third world war. Let us be ready to listen patiently when one of them has the kindness to tell us that our efforts do not seem to him to make perfect sense. The essence of his message is this: "The longer you continue to do what you are doing now, the more Communists you will create not only in Vietnam but all over Asia, Africa, and Latin America. Be worried in time!" Or is it already too late?

THOMAS MERTON

VIETNAM
Lotus in a Sea of Fire

I. THE LOTUS IN A SEA OF FIRE

THE WORLD first began to give real consideration to the Vietnamese problem and the role of the Buddhists only after the Venerable Thich Quang-Duc burned himself on Phan-dinh-Phung Street in Saigon on June 11, 1963, to call the attention of the world public to the sufferings of the Vietnamese people under Ngo Dinh Diem's oppressive regime. The Venerable Thich Quang-Duc's self-immolation had a far greater emotional impact on the West than on the East because of the great difference in religious and cultural backgrounds.

On my trip from New York to Stockholm, I met an American woman doctor on the plane. She asked me many questions about Vietnam. Although she agreed with the motives behind the movement to end the Vietnam war, she was quite unable to accept the Venerable Thich Quang-Duc's self-immolation, which seemed to her the act of an abnormal person. She saw self-burning as an act of savagery, violence, and fanaticism, requiring a condition of mental unbalance. When I explained to her that the Venerable Thich Quang-Duc was over seventy, that I had lived with him for nearly one year at Long-Vinh pagoda and found him a very kind and lucid person, and that he was calm and in full possession of his mental faculties when he burned himself, she could not believe it. I said no more, realizing then that she could never understand. She could not understand because she was unable, though not unwilling, to look at the act of self-burning from any angle but her own.

Since then, the world has nurtured many doubts and invented a great many hypotheses about the Buddhists in Vietnam. Most Westerners have very little knowledge of what seems to them a strange unorthodox religion. They tend to accept the stereotype of "monks" as uneducated, superstitious indigents who shave their heads, forgo meat, and recite prayers for salvation from rebirth. Some see them as having caused trouble and disorder in South Vietnam, and hindered the war against the Communists. For these people, the monks seem to be either men ambitious for power or

1

dupes of the Communists, or, perhaps, simply naïve in the belief that they can cope with the Communists, as a sheep might think it could outwit a wolf.

A numbers game became popular, with guesses about the percentage of Buddhists among the population of South Vietnam, and full of efforts to distinguish practicing Buddhists from nominal ones, militants from moderates. In the end, however, most people do not seem to get very far in their understanding of Vietnamese Buddhism, and consequently they cannot comprehend the Vietnamese problem. It is, in fact, a complex matter to which easy answers are impossible and simple formulations misleading.

Early in 1966, I met an Italian reporter in Saigon. He told me that, after the first few days at Hue, he had felt quite able to understand the nature and meaning of the struggle in the clash of students and others in Hue and Danang. But then he said that the more deeply he inquired into it, the less clear it became to him, and that when he finally left the former imperial city two weeks later his mind was in a state of utter confusion. The fact is that even those who live in Saigon and Hue have much difficulty in grasping what has happened; why not then a foreigner such as he who knows hardly anything about Vietnam? Furthermore, spies of all sorts abound in Vietnam and our reporter may well have been mistaken for a foreign agent, which would have cut him off from reliable sources of information. Not long before, I myself had traveled to Hue. I am a native of Vietnam and have been associated with Buddhism here for twenty years, yet it took all of five days in Hue to search out the nature and objectives of the struggle movement. Even then, I had to work hard to be able to answer questions that bothered our friend the foreign reporter later in Saigon.

After twenty years of war, Vietnamese society now approaches the ultimate in disintegration. The needless killing and dying that occur every day, the destruction of property, and the venal use of money to erode human values have resulted in widespread doubt and frustration among the Vietnamese. Nearly everyone is prey to venality, so that money seems able to purchase women, politicians, generals, and intellectuals alike. In such a situation the peasants, who constitute up to 90 per cent of the country's population, turn for help to their religious leaders. They, then, in turn, are all but forced to act: the Buddhist population may often be found complaining about their spiritual leaders' silence in the face of the nation's suffering.

In a river current, it is not the water in front that pulls the river along, but the water in the rear that acts as the driving force, pushing the water in front forward. The image may serve to explain the engagement of the Unified Buddhist Church in worldly affairs, and help to reveal the nature of reality in present-day Vietnam. Objective conditions in Vietnamese society have compelled the Buddhist religion to engage itself in the life of the nation. To explain that engagement otherwise, as by the militancy and ambition for power of a few monks, leads to tragic oversimplification of the whole matter.

For this reason, what follows is an outline of the history and nature of Vietnamese Buddhism, together with a survey of the relationships between it and other social realities present in this country. Only against this background can the role of the Buddhists in Vietnam be understood and evaluated.

II. THE HISTORICAL SETTING

Vietnamese Buddhism

THIEN, THE VIETNAMESE ZEN

THE HISTORY of Vietnamese Buddhism spreads over the eighteen centuries since Buddhism was introduced into Vietnam through two ways: by sea from India and by road from China. At first, Buddhism came into the country along with the Chinese and Indian merchants. However, Buddhist works dating from the thirteenth and fourteenth centuries recorded the presence of foreign monks in Giao Chau (present-day North Vietnam) from as early as the second century A.D. Giao Chau was then the rest station for Buddhist missionaries traveling by sea between India and China and vice versa.

From the second century A.D. to the tenth century two popular sects among the population of Giao Chau were the A-Ham (Agama) and the Thien (Dhyana). Gradually the Thien sect became dominant and later gave rise to other native sects and subsects.

In the history of Vietnamese Buddhism, Thien (in Sanskrit, Dhyana; Chinese, Ch'an; and Japanese, Zen) is by far the most important sect. The practice of Thien is by no means easy. It requires a profound and powerful inner life, long and persistent training, and a strong, firm will.

The attitude of Thien toward the search for truth and its view of the problem of living in this world are extremely liberal. Thien does not recognize any dogma or belief that would hold back man's progress in acquiring knowledge or in his daily life. Thien differs from orthodox religions in that it is not conditioned by any set of beliefs. In other words, Thien is an attitude or a method for arriving at knowledge and action. For Thien the techniques of right eating and drinking, of right breathing and right concentration and meditation, are far more vital than mere beliefs. A person who practices Zen meditation does not have to rely on beliefs in hell,

4

nirvana, rebirth, or causality; he has only to rely on the reality of his body, his psychology, biology, and his own past experiences or the instructions of Zen Masters who have preceded him. His aim is to *attain,* to *penetrate,* to *see;* once he has attained *satori* (insight) his action will conform by itself to reality.

Thien is one of the many sects of Mahayana Buddhism, which is widely practiced in China, Japan, Korea, and Vietnam. Mahayana Buddhism belongs to the progressive school and is ever ready for change or metamorphosis and for adapting to and accepting the cultural and social conditions of every land and every time. On the other hand, Southern or Theravada (Hinayana) Buddhism, such as is found in Ceylon, Burma, Thailand, Laos, and Cambodia, belongs to a more conservative school.

In Vietnam, the growth and development of Hinayana Buddhism took place very late in the country's history. Although it was introduced in the early centuries of Vietnamese Buddhism, it took root much later in the southern part of Vietnam where many people of the Khmer race live. Economic and cultural exchanges between Cambodia and Vietnam considerably contributed to the spread of Southern Buddhism, mostly in South Vietnam and also in some areas in central Vietnam.

Although Southern Buddhism is practiced by a minority in Vietnam, it performed an outstanding feat, unmatched anywhere else in the world, when it joined hands with Northern Buddhism in a Unified Church. This history-making unification was achieved at the Buddhist National Congress held late in 1963, after the overthrow of the government of Ngo Dinh Diem. It may well serve as an example for a World Unified Buddhist Church in the future.

In Vietnam there are many Zen monasteries, where monks learn the theories and practices of Buddhism under the guidance of Zen Masters. Some of these have hundreds of monks in residence. After their studies and training these monks are appointed to small pagodas, to continue their monastic life or to take care of the faithful in the villages or districts. There are also several nunneries for the Bikkhunis.

In almost every village throughout Vietnam, there is a village common house (*dinh*) and a pagoda (*chua*). The village common house is both the chapel where the villagers worship their titular god, who is supposed to be the protector of the village, and the meeting hall of the village. The pagoda, on the other hand, is the place where the villagers worship Buddha. Its care is in the hands of one of its several monks. The village people attend the pagoda on the first and fifteenth days of the lunar month and bring flowers and joss sticks with them for paying homage to the Buddha. They also go to the pagoda on the evenings of the fourteenth and thirtieth days of the month to repent for wrongs done and to make vows to do right.

The small village pagoda often does not have a well-qualified Zen Master, since most people, and in particular the villagers, cannot practice Zen as taught in the monastery. This must be performed by qualified monks and possibly by a few educated laymen. For this reason popular Buddhism in Vietnam is a mixture of some basic Zen elements and many practices of the Pure Land (Amidist) sect, which is a sect of Mahayana Buddhism that is very popular among the masses.

The practice of the Pure Land sect consists essentially in achieving concentration of the mind through self-absorption and reciting the names of the Buddha. The person who practices Amidism has to keep five precepts: abstention from killing, abstention from acts of banditry and theft, abstention from wrong sexual practices, abstention from lying, and abstention from wrong speech and intoxicants. He has to recite the Amitabhasutra and the name of the Amitabha Buddha. He also is expected to perform right actions so as to gain merit for himself or for his relatives. The merits he accumulates by performing good deeds will make his present life joyful and happy, and will deliver him to the land of absolute joy, or Buddha Amitabha's "Pure Land," after his death.

According to the Pure Land school, this world is an ideal place for study and practice toward the attainment of total liberation. The people who live in this world are instructed and guided by the Amitabha Buddha whose name (Amitabha) means "immeasurable light and immeasurable time."

Basing their teaching on the essay on the Amitabhasutra by the great monk Van The, the Vietnamese Zen Masters have thus realized a synthetic doctrine combining Zen and the Pure Land practices that suits the masses of the people. Except for the pure Zen monasteries, almost every pagoda in Vietnam practices this combined Zen-Pure Land doctrine. In Saigon, for example, there is a large pagoda called Temple of the Zen-Pure Land School, or Thien Tinh Dao Trang. When we talk about the village pagoda and its monk, therefore, we think of this school.

BUDDHISM AND NATION BUILDING

When Chinese characters were first brought to Vietnam, few Vietnamese learned them, with the exception of the Zen Masters, who had to cultivate a knowledge of this ideographic language in order to be able to read the Tripitaka, or Triple Baskets of Buddhist texts. Thus it came about that those monks were the best men of letters in the country. Thanks to their knowledge of Chinese characters, they could read books on medicine, astrology, politics, and philosophy, and attain a highly cultured status among the people.

Under the Dinh and Tien Le dynasties (968-1009) the great Zen Master Ngo Chan Luu acted as imperial counselor on political, religious, and cultural matters to King Dinh Bo Linh and other monarchs who succeeded him. The Zen Masters of that time had already begun to think of training a generation of educated leaders to handle the nation's affairs.

The kings' education and training under the Dinh and Tien Le dynasties left much to be desired, and they therefore depended heavily on the monks in the task of building a nation. The latter had little bias in politics, and the population was largely Buddhist. The monks even received the Chinese ambassadors on behalf of the kings. They opened schools to train qualified leaders to establish charitable institutions for the poor and the sick. In addition, Buddhism made its contribution to the nation's wealth in architecture, economics, culture, politics, and morals, and helped Vietnam become a strong and viable country.

In the year 1010, Ly Thai To[1] acceded to the throne and founded the Ly Dynasty, which ushered the nation into a golden era. Vietnam prospered and flourished in the cultural, political, and military fields. This era of prosperity lasted until the end of the fourteenth century.

RELATIONSHIP WITH CONFUCIANISM AND TAOISM

Although Chinese characters were introduced into Vietnam from the first centuries A.D., Confucianism had to wait until the eleventh

---

[1] Ly Thai To's original name was Ly Cong Uan. He was the adopted son of the Venerable Ly Khanh Van, and the disciple of Patriarch Van-Hanh. His Master, Patriarch Van-Hanh, and other Zen Masters had to deploy all their talents and energy to help him and his successors build a strong nation capable of resisting China.

century to establish itself in the country as an institution. The adaptation of Chinese characters to official court literature began in the tenth century. Buddhist laymen and clergymen of the eleventh century, aware that Chinese characters and the political doctrine of Confucianism were needed for building the nation, helped establish the teaching of both. In 1070, King Ly Thanh Ton built The Temple of Literature in the capital of Thang Long, now Hanoi, for the teaching of Chinese characters and Confucianism. Six years later he built Quoc Tu Giam; in 1236, King Tran Thai Tong built Quoc Tu Vien, and in 1253, Quoc Hoc Vien—all places for the training of young people as leaders of the nation. The first teachers in these institutes were Zen monks, who were masters in the knowledge of Confucianism.

There are three types of Confucians in Vietnam: the *hien nho* Confucians who succeed in examinations and become mandarins, having position and authority; the *an nho,* who also have talent and wisdom but are not willing to hold office, secluding themselves instead for the enjoyment of leisure and peace; and the *han nho* who, after failing to pass their examinations, take teaching jobs or practice medicine for a living.

The development of Confucianism in Vietnam came about largely as a result of the institution of competitive examinations for selecting mandarins. In the first stages of the development of Confucianism and the academic educational system that put a great deal of emphasis on letters and degrees, no conflict seems to have arisen between the Confucians and Buddhists. The monarchs of the Tran Dynasty realized that while Buddhism contained a powerful inner life, Confucianism had a political philosophy and a code of conduct necessary for the development of the kingdom. The great King-monk Tran Thai Tong made this clear in his preface to his work *Thien Tong Chi Nam (Guide to Zen).* He tells the readers the story of his abdication and escape to the mountain in search of a guru. After disguising himself as a common man, the king traveled for many days through forest and mountains before reaching the foot of Mount Yen Tu.

The following day, I climbed to the top of the mountain and came to present my greetings to the Venerable Truc Lam,[2] the great monk

[2] The Truc Lam sect on Mount Yen Tu was an effort by the native Zen Masters to create a genuine local school of Zen. Its founder was Tue Trung Thuong Si, a national hero who had taken a leading part in routing the Mongol invaders. Although a layman, he became a great Zen Master

and imperial counselor. When His Eminence saw me, he looked very glad and said with solemn dignity, "I have made my abode in this mountain for a long time and my body has become thin living on a diet of vegetables and fruits, but I enjoy a walk in the woods and the water of the springs and feel as happy and free as the floating clouds that come with the winds. But what has caused your Majesty to abandon your throne as the lord of men to take such a difficult trip to come here in person?"

When I heard these words of His Eminence I could not help crying, and replied: "I am still very young and feel lonely with no one to rely on to help me rule the people, since my parents are gone to the world beyond. Moreover, well aware of the impermanence of glory that has affected the monarchs in the past, I have come here to seek nothing but the path to Buddhahood."

At that, His Eminence advised me: "The Buddha is not in the mountain, but in your very mind. When your mind is calm and clear, Buddha appears. Now, when your Majesty discovers the right nature of the mind then you may attain Buddhahood immediately and do not have to go far to seek it."

This doctrine that Buddha is present in everyone is quite clear in orthodox Buddhist belief.

While the king was holding this conversation with Truc Lam on Mount Yen Tu, Premier Tran Thu Do and other ministers were setting out in pursuit in order to ask him to return to the court. When the premier and his party found the king at Mount Yen Tu, they insisted on his return and begged him not to think of his own salvation but of his responsibility to the country. The premier said: "If your Majesty does not reconsider your decision, my party and I would rather die here than return."

The king thereupon asked Truc Lam's advice. The imperial counselor held his hand, and said: "As a rule, the monarch has to accept the people's will as his own. Now that the people want you to return to the throne, how can you refuse them? However, when you come back to the court, you would do well not to forget the study of the scriptures." On this advice of His Eminence the

---

and was held in high esteem by contemporary students of Buddhism. Even Zen adepts solicited his instruction. His lofty thoughts and noble conduct, reflecting his detachment from the vanity of the world, are revealed to us in some of his writings, such as *Thuong Si ngu luc,* a selection of his sayings that has been preserved and handed down to posterity.

king returned with the premier and his party to the capital and ascended the throne with much reluctance.

So the Buddha is not in the mountain. He is considered to be in everyone, so that the peace and well-being of the whole people require that every Buddhist should fulfill his responsibility to the community while not neglecting his inner life. The notion of "co-operative division of labor" (Phat Thanh Phan Cong Hop Tac) between Buddhism and Confucianism as outlined in the *Guide to Zen* was to serve as the foundation for the later harmonious combination of these two great doctrines.

The great King-monk had this to say:

Buddhahood recognizes no South or North, and everyone, whether ignorant or intelligent, has his share of the ability to insight. Buddhism is the guide of the ignorant and the lens to scrutinize the problem of birth and death in the most crystal-clear fashion, which is the doctrine of Buddha.

On the other hand, the doctrine of the Saint Confucius bears the heavy responsibility of preserving the balance of discipline for future generations. The sixth Patriarch said: "There exists no difference between Buddha and the Saint Confucius." This shows that the doctrine of Buddha needs Confucianism for its perpetuation in the future.[3]

Thus, the great King-monk expressed his intention to give Confucianism the heavy task of translating the sublime spiritual wealth of Buddhism into concrete achievement. His plan to combine the two great doctrines met with a positive response from a number of the monks.

The kings of the Ly and Tran dynasties depended on the monks not for political support but because they realized that the monks' talents and knowledge were vital to the growth of the country. And they also venerated the Buddha's teachings. More than one monarch relinquished the throne in favor of the homeless life of a monk, and engaged in teaching and writing.

Because of its contribution to political philosophy, Confucianism was readily welcomed by the monks in a spirit of co-operation. However, after the competitive examinations had clearly become the way to advance to high position in the administration of the kingdom, most young people chose Confucianism's academic education over that of the Buddhists, which still preserved its character of disinterested learning.

[3] *Guide to Zen,* Tran Thai Tong.

When the Confucians had consolidated their position at court, they began to be aggressive toward the Buddhist monks. These monks always kept to the simple monastic life even though they enjoyed the king's esteem and confidence. As soon as they became aware of the competitive feelings the Confucians harbored against them, the monks simply ceased their visits to the court and remained in the monasteries, guiding and instructing the clergy and the people in Buddha's doctrine. Thus, Buddhism gradually ceded its influence in national politics to Confucianism.

As the younger generation showed its predilection for the academic education of Confucianism, Buddhist study became limited to the clergy. The philosophy of action of Buddhism as initiated and experimented with during the Ly and Tran dynasties never fully materialized before other events swept away its chance.

In 1321, King Tran Hien Ton issued a royal decree establishing an examination for all the monks in the country. This examination tested the monks on the Kimcuong Vajjracchedica Prajnaparamita Sutra, and those who failed it had to return to secular life. In 1381, King Phe De decreed the drafting of the Buddhist clergy into the Royal Expeditionary Corps to fight in Champa. Under these and similar attacks, many talented and virtuous monks withdrew to the monastic life.

Mahayana Buddhism is characterized by a disposition to synthesis, which explains its remarkable flexibility and adaptability to a variety of cultural environments. For this reason, Burmese Buddhism is different from Indian Buddhism, Tibetan Buddhism from Japanese. It is no exaggeration to say that there are as many Buddhist schools as there are socio-cultural milieus.

Buddhism's affinity for synthesis and adaptation is a mark of its tolerance and freedom from dogmatism. Tue Trung Thuong Si's "The Eccentric's Song" illustrates the way in which the spirit of Zen blends with the freedom and aloofness of Taoism and the sense of responsibility of Confucianism:

Nature is immense,
I wander in great freedom,
To the lofty mountains where the clouds hide,
And to the deep waters of the great oceans.
When I am hungry I eat and eat Hoa La meal.
When I am tired, I sleep at the village—village of nowhere.
When I feel like playing music, I use a flute without a hole,

I burn incense of detachment when it is serene,
And I sleep on the ground of delight when I feel tired.
I quench my thirst with a portion of leisure.
At Van-nien village I recite Lao Bang's verses,
And I sing the Thuong Lang refrain on Cuu Khuc river,
I find my way to Tao khe spring to present my greetings to Lo Thi,
I come to see Thach Dau and find my equal to Lao bang,
Let me enjoy my joy—the joy of Bo dai,
Let me enjoy my accentuation—the accentuation of Pho hoa,
Because, listen—wealth and glory are as fleeting as the clouds floating
    in the sky,
Alas! time is going by!
The mandarin career is perilous, why then should I venture in it?
What shall I do then because people are not constant?
One should take off one's clothes to cross deep waters and roll up one's
    clothes to walk shallow waters.
One should offer one's service when called upon but should retire into
    seclusion when wanted.
One should not cling to one's body composed of the four elements,
And attain insight in this very life and cause all wandering.
Thus one fulfills one's vow: to discover one's real home
And to reach beyond the pressure of birth and death.

I have already noted that the more dogmatic elements among
the Confucians did not reciprocate the Buddhists' good will. Taoism, on the other hand, poorly understood and imperfectly practiced by the common people, came to embrace the employment of
magical powers, so that Buddhism's exchange with Taoism on the
popular level is of a different character from the exchange of Zen
Buddhists with Taoist scholars.

Even so, the mass of the people can accept a complete synthesis
of these three doctrines, and Buddhism then becomes the common
denominator in the beliefs of the Vietnamese people. A Vietnamese
who professes to be a Confucian does not deny his belief in Buddhism, nor must a convinced Buddhist declare that he disbelieves
Confucianism. That is why we cannot say with accuracy how many
Vietnamese are Buddhist. When we examine the beliefs of a typical peasant we find elements of Buddhism, Taoism, and Confucianism intimately mixed together, along with still other elements belonging to native beliefs that existed even before the three great
religions were introduced into Vietnam.

DECLINE OF CONFUCIANISM AND TAOISM

Thanks to the recruiting examination instituted by royal decree to select mandarins, Confucianism flourished and held a unique position for many generations, until the nineteenth century when the young and the intellectuals abandoned it for a Western educational system installed by the French and which promised "milk in the morning and champagne in the evening," as the saying went. In the first prosperous days of Western education, the meeting of the mandarins in retirement with the Buddhists could be observed, together with a revival of the intimate friendship that had existed between them earlier. It was commonplace to see these mandarins and scholars of Confucianism engaged in long conversations with the monks in an atmosphere reminiscent of their tea and chess parties of centuries past. As time went on the Confucians withdrew into obscurity.

As for Taoism, it was introduced into Vietnam at about the same time as Confucianism, but it does not have schools and systems as in China. In Vietnam, the essence of Lao Tse's and Tchang Tse's philosophy is expressed only in the thought and conduct of educated persons of both Buddhist and Confucian faith. There were no Taoist clergy as such in Vietnam. Among the ordinary people, there were, however, a number of Taoist practitioners who knew little doctrine but made a living from their supposed magical powers. Although these practices have had a noticeable impact on the lives of the villagers prone to popular superstitions and have led many people to misunderstand Taoism's important points of doctrine, they do not reflect the high spirit and thought of orthodox Taoism.

The establishment of Western educational and examination systems gradually eliminated the political and religious role of Confucianism in Vietnamese society. Today, there are only a few makeshift associations of Confucian studies extant, seeking to preserve the influence of Confucius' thought in a society of rapid change. Although the anniversary of Confucius is celebrated every year, it has become simply a memorial service and does not have the religious character of Wesak and Christmas.

The movement for the revival of Confucianism started at the same time as the movement for the Buddhist revival in the 1920's, but the Buddhist study societies were rapidly brought into the

Buddhist Church while the Confucian study associations remained unchanged and kept to their purposes of study and cultural activity. Thus, the religious character of Confucianism has gradually disappeared and Confucian conduct is identifiable only as it partakes of the local culture. Such Confucian ideas as loyalty and filial piety, humaneness, kindness, gratitude, courtesy, wisdom, and honesty have been taken over and assimilated by Buddhism and combined with their parallels in the latter's philosophy. Thus the notion of filial piety in Confucianism is fully realized and exemplified in the Buddhist Vulan Ullambana Sutra and the ceremony of the "wandering souls" on the full-moon night of the seventh lunar month. The Confucian notion of humaneness has been merged with the Buddhist notion of compassion or loving-kindness. This process of assimilation has gone so far that, at the present time, Confucianism has lost all of its religious character.

Enter Roman Catholicism

Roman Catholicism has been regarded generally as a foreign faith introduced by Westerners, particularly the French, and during all its history in Vietnam has been closely associated with white explorers, with merchants, and ruling classes. A number of sensible Catholics are well aware of this unfortunate accident of history and have tried to minimize the impression it has left in the minds of the population. Within the ranks of the Roman Catholic Church in Vietnam there are many who cherish the same longings and endure the same anxieties as the nation at large. In the hope that the ghosts of the past may cease to trouble the present, we wish to face up here to a number of serious problems inherited from that past.

Any organization, no matter when and where it exists, lives in danger of infiltration by undesirable elements who want to trade in influence. The Buddhist Church suffered severely from this when it was enjoying its era of glory and prosperity. So, too, has the Roman Catholic Church.

The fundamental mistakes were made by Catholic missionaries of centuries past. These overzealous visitors made use of merchants and politicians to assist them in their missionary work and in turn were made use of by the same merchants and politicians who wished to advance themselves. Moreover, the obvious lack of tact and even the fanaticism with which the missionary fathers attacked the traditional religious beliefs and customs of Vietnam produced a violent reaction that caused the missionaries to be suppressed or driven away.

EARLY MISSIONS: RELIGION AND POLITICS

According to the records of the *Kham Dinh Viet Su Thong Giam Cuong Muc* (*Detailed Historical Annals of Vietnam*), the first Catholic missionary to come to Vietnam was Father Ignace, who arrived at Nam-Dinh in 1533. The year 1596 saw the arrival of another Spanish missionary named Diego Avarte. At first the latter obtained from the monarch of the Le Dynasty permission to operate in the North, but later was also allowed by the Nguyen Lords to establish a mission in the South. Soon, however, he had to leave, when the arrival of Spanish warships at Tourane caused Lord Nguyen to suspect him. In 1615, Father Francis Brezonni and four other Jesuits obtained permission for their missions in the South.

Missionary work did not begin its rapid growth, however, until after the establishment of both the Society of Foreign Missions in the South (1615) and the Society of Foreign Missions in the North (1626). An important figure in this work was the scholar-missionary Father Alexandre de Rhodes. Born in Avignon, France, in 1591, he had joined the Jesuit Order in 1612 and seven years later gone to Goa and, later, to Malacca and Macao. Directed by the Vatican to go to Japan, he wound up instead in Vietnam because of Japan's prohibition of Christian missionaries. In 1625 he arrived in the South, and two years later obtained permission to operate in the North, where his diplomatic qualities gained for him the warm regard of the Trinh Lords. By 1630, however, he had come under suspicion of having political links to the Western powers and was expelled from the North.

During the intervening years he had carefully studied the language, history, and geography of Vietnam and, according to Dao Duy Anh in his *History of the Evolution of Vietnamese Civilization,* had placed this knowledge at the disposal of the Western nations. From 1630 to 1640, he taught theology at the Collège des Jésuites in Macao. After that, he returned to the South, but soon was again expelled and in 1649 arrived in Rome. Three years later he established in Paris the Society of Foreign Missions (Société des Missions Etrangères). This society sent its missionaries to

Vietnam in ever-increasing numbers, with the result that the Catholic Church of France became dominant in Vietnam at the expense of the churches of other European powers.

Dao Duy Anh writes:

Around the years 1680 to 1682 the South counted as many as 600,000 Catholics and the North as many as 200,000. However, missionary work was not always easy. Because the missionaries were often forerunners for the imperialists and often interfered with the internal affairs of the country, the administrations in both the South and the North were prone to order the prohibition and persecution of the Catholics.[4]

With regard to the Society of Foreign Missions in Paris, Charles Maybon had this to say:

The history of the Society of Foreign Missions is closely associated with the history of the propagation of French influence in Indochina. One of the society's founders, Pallu, served as a link between the two French and Vietnamese courts. The most illustrious missionary in the society, Bishop Adran Pigneau de Behaine, officially strengthened this tie: the interference of the society's members in Vietnamese affairs led to the first armed interventions.[5]

In his exile, Emperor Gia Long received Father Pigneau de Behaine's help in the attempt to restore his throne and unify the country. Father de Behaine also exerted his influence to obtain France's military assistance for Nguyen Anh to reconquer his empire. After Nguyen Anh ascended the throne in 1802, he let the missionaries propagate their faith freely out of gratitude for their services. But from 1817 on, when the emperor realized the close association between the missions and the imperialists, he became alert to the potential danger which the missionaries brought.

With the advent of Emperor Minh Mang the anti-Catholic movement began. Emperor Minh Mang was a fervent believer in Confucianism, and attached great importance to the worship of the sages and to the cult of the ancestors. While Buddhism tolerated and easily assimilated these practices, Roman Catholicism opposed

---

[4] *History of the Evolution of Vietnamese Civilization (Viet Nam Van Hoa Su Cuong)*, Quan-Hai Publishing House, 1938.

[5] *Histoire Moderne du Pays d'Annam*, Paris, 1920.

them as unthinkable. Not surprisingly, the emperor and the mandarins declared Roman Catholicism to be wrong, and harmful to their country's traditional culture.

At first Emperor Minh Mang used mild measures against the Catholic missionaries, such as concentrating the French missionaries at Hue, the imperial capital, and using them as translators of Western publications or as writers of Western history, in order to limit their activities. Later, however, the emperor resorted to much harsher policies against the Catholics, after he learned of numerous incidents such as the Le Van Khoi Rebellion in Cochinchina (1833), in which a French missionary, Father Marchand, was involved. Then began a series of persecutions against the Catholics during which the missionaries bravely stood their ground and continued their work either openly or in secret.

Emperor Minh Mang and his successors Thieu Tri and Tu Duc shared the same concern: that a misstep might well bring disaster to the country. The European powers were pressing harder and harder for markets and colonies and the inevitable was not long in coming. Warships began to arrive at Tourane to intervene against the imprisonment of the missionaries. Then began the conquest of Vietnam by France. After France completed her conquest of Vietnam, the prohibition of Roman Catholicism ceased, and since then that religion has enjoyed full freedom to propagate its faith. Thus the association of religion with politics is deeply ingrained in the history of the Vietnamese people.

The ill-feeling caused by the Western missionaries who offended traditional religions in Vietnam originated from the missionaries' hostility to the autochthonous culture, its religions and political arrangements. Anyone who takes the trouble to read the sermons the missionaries used to preach can understand why the opposition of the Vietnamese population to Roman Catholicism has a religious and cultural basis. And a survey of the relationship between the Western religion and political activities in Southeast Asia will reveal the reasons that lie behind the political opposition to Roman Catholicism.

In *Catechism in Eight Days,*[6] prepared by Alexandre de Rhodes himself for the use of European missionaries in Vietnam, Father

---

[6] *Catéchisme pour ceux qui veulent réussir le baptême divisé en huit jours,* Alexandre de Rhodes, de la Société de Jésus et missionaire apostolique de cette sacrée Congrégation.

de Rhodes analyzed and criticized the religions in Vietnam, including Confucianism, Taoism, and Buddhism.

As regards the origin of Buddhism, he said:

Let us begin with Buddhism, which originated from India. Its falsehood and untruthful character stem directly from its very source. About 3000 years after the world was created, there was an Indian king by the name of Tinphan who had a very intelligent but arrogant son. At first this young man married the first daughter of the king in the next kingdom and then left his home for the ascetic life without her consent. He practiced magical powers either to gain the admiration of the people or to be able to debate with other demons—nobody knew for sure. He learned from Alala and Calala and his doctrine stood half-way between these two old demons'. These two old demons taught him the atheist religion and gave him the name Thich Ca (or Sakya).

When he preached his atheistic and unorthodox religion to the people, nobody listened to him; he then preached, together with the other two demons, a new religion embellished by legend in order to gain a few followers. He preached rebirth and the worship of idols, regarding himself as the greatest idol, or as God, or the creator and master of the universe. He used fable and his magical powers to madden people and force them to accept the worship of images. He promised those who worshipped idols, even the lowest ones, that they would be reborn into royal families, through the doctrine of rebirth. As for his disciples, he led them to the abyss of atheism, teaching that everything comes from nothing and shall return to nothing.

This religion has two sides. The outer side consists in the impious worship of the images, and, in many fables, chants that lead the people to worship of superstitious idols and to committing of countless sins. The second and inner side is much worse because it is atheism and lets loose all kinds of sins. This is poison. This is why Confucius, the greatest sage in China, denounced the worship of idols, as the religion of the barbarians.

Regarding Buddhism in China, Alexandre de Rhodes wrote:

But you may ask why the cult of the idols could spread to China since this cult originated in India, which the Chinese regarded as very savage and uncivilized. The answer is that the Chinese are obviously much more civilized than the Indian tribes both in the science of the spirit and that of the body. The Indians are very ignorant in science and usually go naked. In his writings, Confucius announced that the future generation should look for a Saint in the West. The Chinese

Emperor Han Minh De read this book and in it found God's advice to seek the true religion in the great West. He therefore sent a great minister in search of the Saint. After a long trip lasting several months, this great mandarin arrived in India, which the Chinese called the western land, although it was only half-way to the great West. The mandarin was very tired and, as the road was still long and difficult, he did not want to go further. He then asked whether there was any religion in India that he could take back to the Chinese Emperor. He was told of Thich Ca's impious religion, which the mandarin was very glad to take back from the great West.

This is clearly a deliberate effort to identify Roman Catholicism with Emperor Han Minh De's dream of the Golden Man. In fact, when Emperor Han Minh De told his mandarins that he had seen a golden man in his dream, they interpreted this to mean the religion of the Tay Vuc (West), that is, India. The party sent by the emperor comprised eighteen members among whom were Thai Ham and Vuong Tuan. This party was sent to India in the year A.D. 67 and invited two great monks to China, Ca Diep Ma Dang and Truc Phap Lan, to translate the Forty-two Chapter Text and sixteen other texts.

Alexandre de Rhodes wrote at the beginning of the chapter in which he refuted the Buddha's teaching:

Just as we would cause every branch and leaf of a great tree to fall when we felled the old and dangerous tree itself, so after we overthrow this black liar, that is Sakya (Buddha), all the legends about the idols that he created would then crumble by themselves.

Preaching in such manner may rapidly win a number of believers (those who have no knowledge of Buddhism would have no love for Buddhism at all should they read these lines), but it also creates violent reactions. This way of preaching sows the seed of more than one religious conflict. Apart from maligning Buddhism, the violently provocative language of the *Catechism in Eight Days* also attacked Confucianism, Taoism, and other beliefs in Vietnam.

Dao Duy Anh gives the following reasons why the influence of Christianity is not so strong in Vietnam:

Most people suspect Christianity and discriminate against it because they believe that Christianity is contrary to our moral and cultural heritage when it does not accept the cult of ancestors. Emperor Minh

Mang's decree prohibiting Roman Catholicism stated: "The wicked religion of the western people cast its malicious spell on the minds of the people, the Catholic missionaries wrong the people's mind, violate the country's good customs and result in a great harm for the nation." [7] This was in general the attitude of most people in Vietnam and in particular of the Confucians regarding Christianity. There is reason to believe that among those who embraced Christianity at that time, most did so in pursuit of their interests and not out of any deep conviction or faith. For this reason one may say that the Christian spirit has much less influence on our people than its material achievements.[8]

Dao Duy Anh perceived the situation pertaining to culture and beliefs but did not dwell on problems of the political order. The people of Vietnam have a history of over three thousand years and have often fought valiantly to defend their independence from invasion from the north. Their sense of national independence is strong and their patriotism has been a great advantage against invading forces, having many times helped defeat the Chinese and Mongolian armies. So the popular belief that Christianity is the religion of the Westerners and was introduced by them to facilitate their conquest of Vietnam is a political fact of the greatest importance, even though this belief may be based on suspicion alone.

In reality, there were many things that caused the suspicions of the Vietnamese people to increase as the days went by. These suspicions appeared in the emperor mandarins of the Nguyen Dynasty down to the uneducated masses. Emperor Gia Long, his successors Emperors Minh Mang, Thieu Tri, and Tu Duc, and the Confucian mandarins and popular masses all suspected the missionaries of having connections with the European imperialist powers. The uneducated villagers believed that Buddhism and Confucianism were the religions of Vietnam whereas Christianity was the religion of the French. In the villagers' simple minds, to embrace Christianity meant to side with the French. Although this belief was wrong, almost every indication of that time—political, social, or cultural— led the villager to this conclusion.

The belief was strengthened by the open support the French accorded to the Roman Catholic Church after they had conquered

---

[7] First Decree against the Roman Catholic religion, as quoted by Dao Trinh Nhat in *Viet Nam Tay Thuoc Su* (*The History of Vietnam under Western Domination*), Saigon, 1937.
[8] *Viet Nam Van Hoa Su Cuong*, Dao Duy Anh.

Vietnam and made it their colony. Catholic churches and missionaries were not restricted by law or regulation in their work, although other religionists were. As late as 1950, traces of religious discrimination persisted in Royal Decree No. 10, issued on August 6, fixing the status of all associations except the Christian missions, which were beyond the reach of the decree.

While Confucianism and then Buddhism associated themselves closely with the Royalist Resistance forces in order to fight the French invaders, Roman Catholics were suspected of collaborating with them. Bishop Puginier tried to convince the French that the most efficacious way to pacify Tonkin was to persuade all Tonkinese to convert to Roman Catholicism: "With the propagation of the Bible and the French language, in less than twenty years, and without having to force anybody, this country will become Christian and part of France." [9]

In their conquest of Vietnam the French had expected the support of the local Catholics but in the end they felt misled. "The only help the Catholics supplied was spies and translators!" [10] The truth is that there were many Catholics who were honest and patriotic and would never lend the French such services. Unfortunately, the Royalist Resistance Movement made a grave blunder in driving a great number of such honest Catholics into the opposition. In 1885, some elements of the French Expeditionary corps, coming from Vinh and Donghoi, killed many innocent people, destroyed the villages, burned down the Buddhist pagodas and other structures, and regrouped the Catholics near the cities. Leaders of the local resistance movements, angered by the destruction of the Buddhist pagodas by some Catholics, ordered the destruction and burning of Catholic churches as a reprisal. The incidents caused indignation among many Catholics and eventually led to their opposition to the Resistance Movement.

COLONIALISM AND RESISTANCE: "THE MONKS' WAR"

Confucianism and Buddhism were at the very core of the Royalist Resistance Movement against the French from 1885 to 1898. In fact, these two religions provided the movement with its moral

---

[9] *Avec la prédication de l'Evangile et l'enseignement de notre langue, avant vingt ans, sans violer personne, ce pays sera Chrétien et français,* quoted by P. Varet in *Les Dieux qui meurent,* Paris, 1932.

[10] *Histoire Culturelle de la Cochinchine Française,* 1883.

and material force. In the first stage, the movement relied heavily on Confucianism for its strength, but as Confucianism became exhausted, the principal force lay in Buddhism. The Buddhist clergy joined hands with the forces of patriotism and continued the resistance against the invaders. In 1898, for instance, the uprising of Vo Tru in Phu Yen province in central Vietnam galvanized the whole country. The French and the court at Hue called this uprising "The Monks' War."

Vo Tru was a Buddhist monk and the disciple of a Zen Master commonly called Master Da Bac, who lived in a grotto on Mount Ba Chan at Chanh Danh village. Though a monk, Vo Tru was also a revolutionary. The uprising was planned with care from 1895 to 1898 and had the participation of the revolutionary Tran Cao Van and other monks. Many people responded, but it failed because its secrecy was violated. Subsequently, the security service searched all local pagodas and arrested a great number of monks. According to author Hanh Son in Cu Tran Cao Van, "monks were confined in every prison in Binh Dinh and Phu Yen provinces." [11]

In the North, near Hanoi, a monk named Vuong Quoc Chinh started a "Party of the Noble Cause" (Nghia Dang). This party operated under the cover of the Thuong Chi Association and had its bases in the pagodas from Nghe An (in central Vietnam) to Bac Ninh (in North Vietnam), where it spread its propaganda among the Buddhist population. Many monks joined this party and proved to be effective in spreading anti-French revolutionary ideas. The fact that the party operated even among the Catholic population and won over many a patriotic Catholic is worthy of attention.

A secret raid on Hanoi planned for the night of December 5, 1898, was regrettably disclosed, giving the Governor-General P. Doumer sufficient time to organize its defense. The signals were thwarted, and the attack was pushed back. But elsewhere the resistance fighters did not know this in time, and consequently their uprising was brutally suppressed. The party collapsed and many were executed or maimed.

In the South, there were also many such movements of resistance. The rural population in the South were fervent in their faith, and the anti-French movements often relied heavily on this.

[11] *Minh-Tan,* Paris, 1952.

Among the many secret anti-French organizations in the South the most important were the Nghia Hoa, the Thien Dia Hoi, the Luong Huu Hoi, and the Nhon Hoa Duong. Faith was the common factor that bound the members of these clandestine organizations together into tightly knit groups, and Buddhism served as the common denominator for them. In fact, Buddhism was the common element of the Cao Dai and Hoa Hao sects, the two most important religious groups in the South, with their own armies eager to fight for the independence of the country. In these organizations, such practices as religious initiation, the use of media, charms and magic appealing to the masses were considered vital to organizational work. The meetings usually were held at night and in the pagodas, with the monks attending.[12]

Georges Coulet, in his book *Les Sociétés Secrètes en Terre d'Annam,*[13] reveals some of the character of these clandestine revolutionary organizations.

If we bear in mind that the various religions existing in Vietnam may differ in their rites but teach the same moral ideal to their followers, then we will realize the strict and formidable unification that religions impose on the secret organizations in Vietnam.

Sometimes the monks who took part in or led the Resistance Movement against the French were captured and interrogated. In 1916, for instance, the French secret service arrested the monk Nguyen Van Xu of Rach Tre pagoda in Vinh Long. Interrogated, the monk replied that his followers' donations were "to pay for his debts" and "to sustain his loved ones" and were by no means destined for the revolutionary De Tham as some had claimed. The French, however, later sentenced him and forty-three others to long prison terms.

Another monk on Mount Cam, Cao Van Long, told his arresters that he was on his regular rounds, "distributing amulets," but he was charged by the French secret service with serving as liaison between the revolutionary organizations.

In Tam Bao pagoda the secret service discovered another revolutionary organization. The Abbot Dong, many other monks, and a great number of the persons involved were arrested and tortured. Consequently, the Rach Gia Buddhist Study and Mutual Help As-

[12] *Les Sociétés Secrètes en Chine,* Jean Chesneaux (René Julliard, 1965), chapter "Contre La France en Indochine."
[13] Librairie Ardin, Saigon, 1925.

sociation and the Buddhist publication *Tien Hoe* collapsed. Later, Abbot Dong was deported to Con Dao, the ill-famed penal island, and died there. There were countless similar cases.

From the start, the French supported and trusted the Catholics. After the above incidents, which further confirmed the association of Confucianism and Buddhism with the Resistance Movement against French domination, the French had further reason to suspect these two religions and to put their trust in the Catholics alone. This was the beginning of religious discrimination, an idea that cannot be separated from the whole complex drive toward national independence.

Professor Nguyen Van Trung of Saigon University's Faculty of Letters, one of the best-known members of the Catholic intelligentsia, has asserted that the way of life followed by Vietnamese Catholics differs greatly from that of the local population generally —and causes them to appear alienated from the country's life. He wrote:

A number of foreign missionaries misconceived their role and created among their converts a colonial mentality and a negative attitude toward their own civilization. Consequently, their imitation of the mother country has led to the slighting of the local values and practices. A quick look at the local Roman-Gothic churches, which are awkward and grotesque copies of their European counterparts, at the religious ikons, and at the practices of the faithful themselves will suffice to show us the Western character of the Vietnamese Roman Catholic Church. Thus, our form of worship, our art, our religious practices have turned us into strangers among the non-Catholic population. The Roman Catholic Church in Vietnam has become a distinct community, isolated and closed to the other communities in the nation because, when a Vietnamese converts, he not only has to abandon his traditional religion and ancestor worship to accept the Catholic faith, but also to relinquish his native cultural heritage, with which he may assert his Vietnamese identity, all in order to accept a new way of thinking and living and a new set of alien customs. In the end, the Catholics had to live as foreigners amid their countrymen.[14]

Father Pham Han Quynh wrote in 1952 in the journal *Mission*:

The Vietnamese Catholic Church is but the French Church abroad if not the Spanish Church abroad or the Canadian Church overseas. Why?

[14] *Nhan Dinh I,* Nguyen Van Trung, Nam Son, Saigon.

Today, people could not afford to ignore the "made-abroad" character of the Vietnamese Church, not only when they noticed the too small number of Vietnamese bishops after several hundred years of church history with all the key posts and functions in the hands of the foreign missionaries, but also when they noticed the speech and writing style of the Church, its music, its theology and philosophy etc. The fact is that the Vietnamese Catholics are not living amid the Vietnamese society.[15]

The foreign missionaries' misconception of their role, as exposed by Professor Nguyen Van Trung and Father Quynh, is an important reason for the gap between the Catholics and non-Catholics, but apart from this there are other wrong and tactless acts deserving discussion.

The attitude of the early missionaries toward the traditional native culture and religion and the language used to express that attitude caused much strife and destruction. Later this situation was worsened when a number of Catholics showed their dependence on and alliance with the colonial government and then the Ngo Dinh Diem regime. The influence of the Catholic clergy, in particular the French priests, was all too obvious under the French Occupation and even throughout the Indochina war (1946-54). Anyone in trouble, particularly political trouble, could find a safe haven if he asked for the local priest's intervention. Arrests and threats were commonplace under French rule, especially after the return of French troops to Indochina. Under these conditions, the protection and guarantee of safety by the priest was a great source of security. Many people converted to Roman Catholicism out of gratitude for the father's service of this nature. But many had to convert because they had no other choice.[16]

No Vietnamese could help trembling at the memory of the terror as perpetrated by the French army and secret service at that time. This terror, with the deportations, arrests, and tortures that accompanied it, did not cease when the French withdrew from

---

[15] *Informations Catholiques Internationales,* No. 188, page 23.

[16] In *Viet Nam Van Hoa Su Cuong (History of the Evolution of Vietnamese Civilization)* by Dao Duy Anh, completed and published in 1938, we read: "Among those who embraced Christianity . . . most did so in pursuit of their self-interests and not out of any deep . . . faith." Even from 1954 to 1963, many converted to Roman Catholicism just to seek protection, to avoid suspicion, to be left alone, and to avoid being labeled Viet Minh or Viet Cong.

45138

LIBRARY
College of St. Francis
JOLIET, ILL.

Vietnam. It continues to the present and much of the former machine remains, although in different hands.

President Ngo Dinh Diem, a Catholic, was accused of creating a police state. The mobilization of the police forces to suppress the opposition destroyed every chance of democracy. Moreover, the use of this machine to consolidate the political position of the Ngo family and to spread the Catholic religion caused many people to look upon the regime as their enemy.

At the end of 1954, nearly 800,000 refugees, mostly Catholics, left their homes in North Vietnam to come to South Vietnam. The refugee camps and settlement centers received special care from the regime. The Catholic refugees were the regime's favorite citizens, and it was not long before their use of this favoritism caused much ill-feeling among the local population.

The Catholic publication *Informations Catholiques Internationales,* published in Paris, carried in its issue of March 15, 1963, a study on Roman Catholicism in Vietnam which spoke of the "extraordinary progress" of Christian missions under the regime of President Ngo Dinh Diem. The article quoted the priest of Phu Hoa parish in Qui Nhom as saying:

In 1958, Phu Hoa counted 692 Catholics, in 1959 the number had reached 2,000. As for those receiving instruction preparatory to baptism (catechumens) they are countless. Archbishop Ngo Dinh Thuc told me that at Vinh Long diocese, a number of entire villages asked to be baptized collectively. But there are not enough instructors to take care of them. Apart from the Philippines, Vietnam is the only country in the Far East to approach total conversion.

Archbishop Ngo Dinh Thuc was the brother of the late president Ngo Dinh Diem and everyone in Vietnam knew of his power and influence. The above publication also carried a picture of his welcome at Phu Bai airport in Hue, in which may be seen great numbers of soldiers and officers forming a guard of honor. It seems that the archbishop did not pursue solely the achievement of the religious spirit but aimed at the expansion of the influence and power of religion in close association with the consolidation of the regime.[17]

[17] The situation was not unlike what happened in 1964 and 1965 when the influence of Buddhism was at its peak. At that time the Vien Hoa Dao or headquarters of the Buddhist Church was haunted by a great number of persons who were out to trade on the influence of the Buddhist Church and

It is quite true that the use of religion by politics is always accompanied by the pressure of religion on politics. At Quang-Tri, for instance, Archbishop Ngo Dinh Thuc built the center Our Lady of La Vang, a place of pilgrimage situated about thirty kilometers south of the seventeenth parallel. The archbishop called this center "the spiritual bastion of the country," and elevated it to the rank of a basilica. The first issues of the publication *Our Lady of La Vang,* which appeared in 1962, carried the list of the benefactors who had donated for the construction of this center. Topping the list was the vice-president of the republic, Nguyen Ngoc Tho, and after him came a succession of secretaries of state and generals, each donating nearly the same amount. Catholics and non-Catholics alike had to have their names on the list. Lottery tickets to support the La Vang center were given into the care of the traffic police, who forced them on the drivers of buses and private and passenger vehicles, when they violated various traffic rules. Throughout the inauguration of the La Vang center, the state railway fare was reduced by half for pilgrims traveling by groups to La Vang.

The Vinh Long Personalist Philosophy Center is a place where the Diem regime put forward the personalist philosophy, built upon the tenets of Emmanuel Mounier's doctrine, as the answer to communism. This center was started by the archbishop when he was still Bishop of Vinh Long. All public servants, Catholic and non-Catholic alike, had to receive training in this doctrine at the Vinh Long center. Most of the teaching and training staff were priests and bishops. Any trainee who showed any opposition to the doctrine during the course was closely watched, and later punished or dismissed on return to his post. Other examples of the misuse of power to force and punish innocent people occurred in different places, particularly in central Vietnam.

In 1957, the government ordered the abolition of the Buddha Anniversary, or Wesak, as an official holiday in the year. Since this anniversary is as important to the Buddhists as Christmas to the Christians, the Buddhist population became indignant and held the greatest Wesak ever organized. One year later, under the

leaders. Venerable Thich Tam Chau, then head of the Buddhist Vien Hoa Dao (commonly known as Council for Secular Affairs), told me that many people had requested his favors on miscellaneous matters. I told him frankly that if he and the other leaders of the Church allowed themselves to acquiesce in these requests then the Buddhist Church would tread the old path used by Christian missionaries.

pressure of the Buddhists throughout the whole country, the government had to reverse its decision and recognize the event as a national holiday.

During the Buddhist crisis in 1963, the Overseas Vietnamese Buddhist Association received from Saigon an important and voluminous document on these cases of persecution. In the middle of 1963, all the delegations to the United Nations organization in New York received from the Overseas Vietnamese Buddhist Association a Remonstrance of forty-nine pages in which were exposed in detail the violations of human rights and the discrimination against the Buddhist population by the regime of Ngo Dinh Diem. At the end of September, 1963, another document of nearly one hundred pages was sent to the United Nations organization. This document consisted of petitions, depositions, and reports on forcible arrests and persecutions of the Buddhist population. These papers had the particular names and signatures and seals of the persons and local Buddhist organizations concerned.

According to this document, there were in the province of Quang Ngai alone seven cases in which the local administration forced Buddhists to receive instruction in the personalist doctrine and to convert to Roman Catholicism, eight cases of the misuse of public power to force the Buddhist population to convert, and one case of falsely accusing a Buddhist monk of Communist affiliation and of arresting and imprisoning him. In the province of Binh Dinh there were seven cases of coercing Buddhist cadres to abandon their homes and property for the government settlement camps in the highlands. These cadres were rich farmers, and not of the unemployed group who were supposed to go to the settlement camps. The document also recorded five cases of misuse of power to coerce the Buddhist population to convert to Roman Catholicism in the province of Binh Dinh. In the province of Phu Yen, there were fifteen cases of forced conversions, three cases of calumny and threatened liquidation directed against the Buddhist population, three cases of arrest, torture, and liquidation, one case of the live burial of two Buddhists in the same tomb.

NATIONALIST CATHOLICISM: A NEW OUTLOOK

While the gap was being widened by the regime, many responsible and well-informed Catholics were worried and worked hard to acquire a really solid and durable foundation in Vietnamese society for the Catholic Church. Even under the regime of President Ngo Dinh Diem, Professor Nguyen Van Trung asserted impartially that "the Catholics . . . live as foreigners amid their countrymen." The sense of responsibility and the efforts of this generation of progressive Catholics are really praiseworthy. They have expressed their view that "in order for the Roman Catholic Church to progress, it should endeavor to adapt itself to the sociocultural milieu of Vietnam." With such progressive and commendable aims, these Catholics on the one hand could further an understanding of their religion among the young and, on the other hand, could gradually transform the religion into a native faith of Vietnam with Vietnamese character and color.

The Tinh Viet Van Doan Club (a literary club), its publication *Van Dan* (*Literary Tribune*), and its publishing house Tinh Viet, under the management of Pham Dinh Khiem, dropped its former ancient Bible style to use a new contemporary style. The Le Bac Tinh Music Club also made efforts in a similar direction. Catholic music began to produce its first compositions in the Vietnamese tradition. Father Ngo Duy Linh became Director of the National Conservatory of Music and Dramatic Art. Father Tran Huu Thanh made close contacts with the students and youth and appeared concerned about the limited understanding of Catholic doctrine among the young.

In 1962, many "study weeks" were organized in the big cities. In Saigon there was a Catholic Study and Discussion Week. At Dalat, the Redemptorists organized a Bible Week. Many other lectures and study sessions were organized at various places, such as the Cu Xa Phue Hung and the Thanh Quan pension for girl students. The publication *Song-Dao* (*Living Our Faith*) bravely discussed such issues as "Religion and the Nation." This publication, run by a group of Catholic intellectuals and teachers, could be said to be the most progressive of the Catholic publications. In France, the Catholic journal *Lien Lac* (*Liaison*) followed the same line. A correspondent wrote to *Lien Lac* from Saigon: "You have expressed what we cannot and dare not say over here. *Lien Lac* has accomplished its mission. . . ." At that time Father Nguyen Ngoc Lan was outstanding among the progressive and open-minded Catholics in France. His writings received a great response in Vietnam. This direction of the Catholic progressive intellectuals is full of great promise for the future of the Catholic Church and should be encouraged and supported.

Apart from these efforts in the educational, cultural, and social domains, there were attempts to assert independent Catholic political attitudes. These were extremely important because they proved that there were many patriotic Catholics who were anxious to fight for national and Catholic independence from any foreign power as much as for the regime of President Ngo Dinh Diem. This has the greatest value because it alone can dissipate the mistaken impression of many Vietnamese that Vietnamese Roman Catholics live and depend on foreign political influence and do not stand in the ranks of the nation.

The non-Catholic population should be aware of the existence of these patriotic and progressive Catholics in order to do away with the deep-rooted antagonisms and to facilitate an understanding and dialogue between the two sides. These endeavors within the Catholic Church, which are aimed at enabling the progressive elements to assume important positions in the Church and to assist the Catholic Church to take positions consonant with the nationalist creed, are as important as the efforts to create favorable conditions within the Buddhist Church to liberate its own progressive elements.

The attitude of the Catholics toward the present war in Vietnam is a very important factor that will have much to do with the prestige of the Catholic Church in the future. During the popular revolt against the regime of President Ngo Dinh Diem there were among the resisters some notable progressives from the Catholic Church. While Archbishop Ngo Dinh Thuc, Primate of Vietnam, aligned himself very strongly with the Diem regime, Archbishop Nguyen Van Binh of Saigon was able to say that as the Church has its limitations so must the state have its limitations. Although Archbishop Binh's position was not strong enough to constitute an actual form of opposition or resistance to the Diem regime, it did reveal an awareness of the difficulties that confronted the Catholic Church in any apparent support for that regime.

By now the war has reached such a state of tragic absurdity that there literally can be no religious conscience that does not speak out against it. Although up to now the Catholic Church has not raised its voice officially against the war, there have been courageous and forthright statements by a number of progressive intellectual younger Catholics. The appeal, on January 1, 1966, of eleven Catholic priests for peace moved the whole population. Not only the Catholic peasants in the villages, who as direct victims of the war applauded the initiative of these eleven priests, but also the Buddhists, whose own patriarch had made his strong statement on peace only nineteen days before, heartily supported their effort. But while the Vietnamese who heard of the appeal widely supported it, the government refused to permit it to be reported in the press, and other members of the Catholic hierarchy turned against the eleven priests and accused them of supporting and strengthening communism.

In fact, the people of Vietnam generally are fed up with the whole absurd war, and if there are those who still fight valiantly in the National Liberation Front, it is because they are convinced it is the only way to secure their independence, and not because of any ideological alignment. Anyone standing for a further extension of the war would not be considered by the people themselves as a part of the Vietnam community or as one who understood or shared its sufferings. The Vatican understands this perfectly, and the Archdiocese of Saigon also. That is why both tried (unsuccessfully) to stop the demonstration organized by a minority of Catholics in Saigon on May 12, 1966. The demonstrators carried signs thanking America and its allies for supplying troops, calling for a final victory over communism, and opposing any calls for a cease-fire. The magazine *Informations Catholiques Internationales* of July 1, 1966, wrote:

> That demonstration was authorized by the Vietnam government but was not approved by the Catholic hierarchy. The Archbishop himself more than once let it be known that he opposed the demonstration.

While the more progressive Catholics in Vietnam speak out in the spirit of religious conscience and of the Vatican Council, there are others who still complain that Pope Paul VI does not understand the situation in Vietnam and should confine his efforts to exclusively religious concerns and leave the secular ones to them. In July, 1966, I had the privilege of meeting with Paul VI, and explaining to His Holiness the situation in Vietnam. I appealed to him to call on the Catholics of Vietnam to work with those of other religious faiths in the search for peace, and so give to the progressive Catholics the kind of support that they need as they follow out their legitimate mission in searching for peace. The prospect of Vietnamese Catholics working co-operatively with

other Vietnamese religious and civil groups in a profoundly pro-
Vietnamese way would be immensely encouraging not only for the
Catholics themselves but also for the Buddhists.[18]

Buddhism and Nationalism in Southeast Asia

The renaissance of Buddhism in Southeast Asia has coincided
with the struggle for independence from the great Western powers
by the small nations of that area. Opposition to communism within
Buddhism has been a development of the past ten or fifteen years,
but resistance to Western imperialistic domination is a matter of
the past several centuries. The alliance of Buddhism with nationalistic patriotic forces resisting the French in Vietnam had its
counterpart in similar alliances with nationalistic movements in
other countries in Southeast Asia. The factor of nationalism in the
small countries of Asia and Africa is an immensely important
one, but it must be understood in its true character, as a manifes-
tation of resistance on the part of these countries to conquest and
domination by foreign powers, not as a form of extreme chauvin-
ism. As the problem of nationalism in Vietnam is related to the
problem of nationalism in other Southeast Asian countries, so
the problem of Buddhism in Vietnam is related to that of Buddhism in the other countries. That is why an all-embracing look

[18] The idea of making Buddhism a state religion as it was in the Ly and
Tran dynasties has become for all intellectual Buddhists, clergy and laymen,
ridiculously out of date, but it still frightens some Catholics. This is seen
clearly in the apprehension of some Catholics over the fact that the headquarters of the Unified Buddhist Church takes the name Viet Nam Quoc Tu,
which can be translated either as the Pagoda of the Country of Vietnam,
or the National Pagoda of Vietnam. In fact, in taking the name Viet Nam
Quoc Tu the Buddhists were only reflecting their feeling that this was the
most important pagoda in the nation, and in no sense attempting to suggest
the renaissance of Buddhism as a state religion.

Curiously enough, many Buddhists are perturbed when Catholics use the
expression Cong Giao to describe their religion, since "Cong" imputes the
meaning of "official." In fact, the expression Cong Giao means only Catholicism, but since the word Cong standing alone means "official" there are
Buddhists who have the apprehension that Catholics want to make their
religion the official one while Buddhism and other faiths become private
religions! Misunderstandings of this sort have to be dissipated. The nation
is in a state of upheaval and on the brink of destruction because of the war,
and Catholics and Buddhists alike must realize that the problem of survival
takes pre-eminence and that understanding and communion between them
is essential now.

at the situation of Buddhism in Southeast Asia will help in the understanding of the situation in Vietnam itself.

Western scholars of an earlier generation, in studying Buddhism, tended to concentrate on the philological aspects of it and to neglect the philosophical content of Buddhism and especially its impact on the societies of which it is a part. Where they have engaged in a study of the philosophy of Buddhism, they have depended upon a limited number of manuscripts to devise a simple system of doctrine, and have failed to put this into the context of the relationship of that doctrine to the life of the people who have adopted Buddhism. Many of them concluded that Buddhism was simply a matter of idol worship and such unlikely superstitions as reincarnation. Only as a few careful scholars began to penetrate the reality of Buddhism did the West begin to entertain a respect for this religion. Some of these scholars, including several Christians, discovered the profound content in Buddhist philosophy and have tried to demonstrate to the West the relationship between it and Christianity. Among them have been scholars whose admiration of the Buddha and for the philosophy of Buddhism have been so great as to lead them to turn to Buddhism themselves. And as these Western scholars discovered a respect for the content and philosophy of Buddhism, so Buddhists themselves began to rediscover the profundities of their own faith. A kind of new faith was born in them, and the renaissance of Buddhism, thanks to that fact, has moved apace. Thus it has been these later Western scholars who have helped markedly in the revitalization of the Buddhists' faith in their own religion.

CEYLON

If Buddhism in such countries as Ceylon and India has demonstrated a new vigor, it is considerably due to the work of such scholars as Sir Edwin Arnold and Henry Steel Olcott. Olcott (1832-1902) was an American who encouraged David Hewavitarane, a formerly Christian Ceylonese who returned to the Buddhist faith of his father, to undertake the revival of Buddhism in Ceylon. David Hewavitarane, who was later ordained as a Buddhist monk under the name the Venerable Dharmapala, meaning the Protector of the Law, did indeed become a protector of Buddhism in both India and Ceylon. When Dharmapala read in the *London Daily Telegraph* in 1885 a series of articles by the poet

Edwin Arnold deploring the deterioration and neglect of the great monuments of Buddhism, especially the Bodhigaya, the place where the great Buddha received his enlightenment, he resolved to restore the vitality of Buddhism in Ceylon and India. All his life Dharmapala tried to realize that vow. Not only were Buddhist monuments restored throughout India, but many new Buddhist institutes, seminaries, magazines, and organizations like the Mahabodhi were established. This revitalization of Buddhism in India has led to a renaissance in literature, art, and social reform.

The thought of both Rabindranath Tagore and Mahatma Gandhi was penetrated by the ideas of Buddhism. The paintings of such artists as Nandalal Bose and Tagore were greatly influenced by the Buddhist paintings in the caves of Ajanta. In social thought one could recall also the example of Dr. Ambedkar, leader of the untouchables or Harijan class. Inspired by the refusal of Buddhism to accept the concept of class discrimination, Dr. Ambedkar at one time led 500,000 Indians of the untouchable class to become Buddhists. This happened at Nagpur, October 14, 1956. Though Dr. Ambedkar died in 1958, this group of Buddhists continued to increase in numbers and strength. Dr. Ambedkar maintained that of all the world religions Buddhism was best suited to respond to the needs of man in the new society.

Ceylon is a country that has been predominantly Buddhist since the third century B.C. In the sixteenth century the Portuguese invaders brought in both Christianity and Western law. In the seventeenth century the Dutch succeeded the Portuguese and pursued the same kind of policy. Around the end of the eighteenth century, when the Netherlands were having their own difficulties at home, the British pushed them out of Ceylon and by 1815 had established their own domination of the island.

All of these Western colonizers pursued a policy of attempting to convert the local population to Christianity, and each time that one of the colonial powers lost its hold on Ceylon, many Ceylonese returned to the traditional Buddhism of their past. But the British, when they took power, demonstrated a very determined missionary effort to convert the entire island. Under British rule, the Buddhist Church lost virtually all of its rights. Governmental decrees deprived the Buddhists of monasteries, gardens, and other institutions, while establishing procedures that favored the Christian missionaries. Although a Declaration in 1815 guaranteed the rights and freedom of worship of the Buddhists, the policy of anti-Buddhist discrimination was persistently followed. Decree No. 10 of 1958, for example, relating to control of temples and monasteries, in fact made it possible for the government to take from the Buddhists a very considerable portion of their lands and buildings. In Kandy district alone, 202,000 acres taken from the Buddhists were turned over to the British colonialists. Thus the Buddhist Church shared its people's experience of being victimized by the colonialists, and was consequently intimately a part of the national resistance movement that grew up among the Ceylonese against the British. Here again, as in Vietnam, there developed a natural affinity between the nationalist and patriotic aspirations of the people and their traditional religion of Buddhism, and Dharmapala was looked upon not only as a prophet of Buddhism but also as a great patriotic leader.

In *Buddhism or Communism, Which Holds the Future of Asia?* [19] Professor Ernst Benz says:

Ceylonese nationalism and Buddhism joined hands all the more readily because of British policy. In the course of various uprisings against the Colonial government, the British military tribunals had to condemn prominent Buddhist monks to death.

When Ceylon gained its independence, the new government guaranteed the freedom of the Buddhist Church. The first premier, Mr. Bandaranaike, who had been converted to Christianity at an early age, had re-embraced Buddhism on his return from his studies in England, adopted national dress, and become active both in the effort for a renaissance of Buddhism and for independence of his country.

BURMA

In Burma, although the British occupation was shorter, the policy of using Christianity as a wedge to divide the people was even clearer, and more brutally demonstrated. The British invasion of Burma began in 1824; by 1855 the whole of Burma had been conquered. Again in Burma, the Buddhists from the very beginning joined hands with the anti-British resistance movement. The British ended the traditional protection of the Buddhist Church by the king. Exactly as in Ceylon, the pagodas and monasteries

[19] Allen and Unwin, Ltd., London, 1966.

were violated, the monks terrorized, and lands were taken away from the Buddhist Church, while the activities of the Buddhists were severely circumscribed. Again the Buddhist monks, of the Hinayana tradition as in Ceylon, were active in the resistance movement before 1886 and in the uprising that occurred in 1931. A Burmese monk named U Wisera, who took part in the resistance and in protesting against the restrictions on the Buddhist Church, was imprisoned by the British in 1929. He died after a hunger strike that lasted more than a hundred days, and following his death was venerated by the whole Burmese population as a martyr. His memory is enshrined in Burma's biggest pagoda, the Swedagon.

Readers will not miss the striking parallel between the activities and experience of U Wisera and those of Vietnam's highly venerated Thich Tri Quang, who risked death in a fast of a hundred days in protest against the domination of his country by a foreign-supported puppet government. The similarity is also seen, of course, by Buddhists throughout the whole of Asia.

All Burmese learn in infancy the story of the huge bell of the Swedagon pagoda. It weighed forty tons and was donated to the pagoda by King Tharravaddi. In 1841, when the British occupied Rangoon, they sought to take the bell to Calcutta, but the raft carrying the bell down the river sank under the heavy weight and the bell disappeared into the depths. Although the British tried every means of recovering it, they were unsuccessful. But the Buddhists, later on, organized themselves into so effective a salvage operation that they were able to recover the bell and take it back to the Swedagon pagoda. The incident seemed to the Burmese to demonstrate that the Buddha was on their side and that they were capable of eventually defeating the British and restoring their independence. Nationalism and Buddhism again had become one.

The identification of Buddhism with nationalism was also reenforced by the fact that the British brought their religion with them at the time they began the conquest of Burma. Their efforts at colonizing included a major effort to convert some of the minority groups, especially the Karens. Some of these minority groups were very open to the preaching of the missionaries, partly because they themselves had been the victims of discriminatory treatment by the Burmese majority. By 1921 some 180,000 Burmese were Christians, but among that number 70 per cent were Karens. After independence the Karens established a separatist movement in an attempt to create a nation of their own, and there was a major uprising in 1949. The reaction of the Burmese was to assume that the separatism of the Karens stemmed from their Christianity, and that they had been urged into such action by the British. The phenomenon is very similar to the situation of the Fulro[20] in the mountains of central Vietnam.

In 1946 the British had to grant independence to Burma, and the Buddhists became the inspiration for the establishment of a non-Communist form of socialistic society headed by U Nu and his associates.

(It should be noted that this attempt to trace the political and sociological effect of the introduction of Christianity into these predominantly Buddhist nations is no reflection on the personal devotion and selfless concern for the people of many of the Christian missionaries who worked in these countries. That is too well known to be argued, and in many cases their own contribution to the colonization of these countries was entirely without their conscious realization.)

COMPARISON OF WESTERN
AND COMMUNIST-CHINESE ATTITUDES

In other countries of Southeast Asia the same phenomenon of the alliance of Buddhism and nationalism has been very clearly seen. In the strength of the various nationalist movements, Buddhism is an important element, and its potentialities for guiding the development of new societies need to be explored more fully than they have been. The West has never recognized this, but instead, when it looks at Buddhism, tends to make a comparison between its subtle and ingrained relationship to the people and the highly organized, highly structured organization of such religions as Catholicism. The Christian missionaries are far better in terms of organization than the local Buddhist institutions. The extensive Western resources behind them make it possible for them to establish impressive schools, hospitals, and other forms of social organization. They come prepared to learn local dialects, are often equipped with the findings of modern psychology, and have access to modern means of communication for the dissemination of their message. A superficial comparison of these highly organized activities with the local Buddhist structure is likely to convince the

[20] Letters that stand for the name, in French, of the United Front for the Struggle of Oppressed Races (Front Uni de Lutte des Races Opprimées).

observer that Buddhism has no future. But when one goes more deeply, one discovers that the strength of Buddhism does not lie in organization, but in the deep roots of the psychological and moral values held by the people.

Ernst Benz has reason behind him when he says: "Buddhism is a religion that shapes the lives of the entire people, or a large part of it; which dictates conduct in all spheres and in all social classes." Benz is not speculating from an ivory tower, but has traveled extensively and has gained personal experience in Buddhist countries, especially in Southeast Asia. His idea is that examination of the organization does not disclose the real strength of Buddhism.

The living spiritual force of Buddhism cannot be so easily grasped—statistically least of all. It represents more a spiritual fluid, an inner attitude, a disposition, than a specific program, let alone ideology.[21]

As one of those connected with the Viet Minh, who went from South Vietnam to North Vietnam in 1954, remarked to the regional post of the Viet Minh, Buddhism is pervasive but formless. For that reason it is difficult to crush. It has its organizations that are simple to shatter, but Buddhism itself remains. It is like a drop of mercury: you can strike the mercury and it will disintegrate into many smaller parts, but as soon as you remove your fist they all run together again.

The Western powers have never adequately recognized this, but tend to underestimate the potential of Buddhism because they judge on their own much more formalistic criteria. In this it must be said that they are less clever than Communist China, which recognizes the importance of Buddhism and has developed a much more intelligent attitude toward it. This is easy to understand, since Orientals can always understand each other better than Westerners can understand them. In the beginning of the Communist regime in China there were some early efforts to suppress the Buddhists, but the Chinese quickly realized the futility of this and adopted much more moderate attitudes that sought to win the support and co-operation of the Buddhists. This is seduction, of course: it does not reflect any illusions on the part of the Communists that the Buddhist philosophy is similar to their own, but represents an attempt to exploit the sympathy of the Buddhists in their op-

[21] *Buddhism or Communism, Which Holds the Future of Asia?* London, 1966.

position to Western powers and to eliminate possible sources of resistance to their own regime.

The General Assembly of the Chinese Buddhists held in Nanking in 1947 gave birth to the Chinese Buddhist Association. According to the report given by the Chinese delegation to the Third Buddhist Conference at Rangoon in 1954, they had at that time in the Association 263,125 members with some four and a half million followers. They operated eleven high schools, eleven advanced institutes, six libraries, and three publishing houses. There are eight Buddhist magazines, including *Modern Buddhism,* printed in Chinese and English. In 1956, a Chinese Buddhist institute was installed in Peking, with a number of Buddhist scholars to carry on studies of Buddhist culture and to care for Buddhist activities in China. The Buddhist publishing house Ching Ling in Nanking had 120,000 block plates, and was allowed to resume the printing of Buddhist scriptures. Buddhist scholars in the institute were permitted to co-operate in the preparation of the Buddhist encyclopedia prepared by Professor Malalasekera. The biggest Buddhist monuments have been carefully restored in China. The Chinese Buddhist Association has sent delegations to Buddhist conventions in other countries in order to report on the state of Buddhism in mainland China. Before 1961, delegations of Japanese Buddhists visited China and were received very warmly. Upon their return, these delegations were full of praise for what they had seen of Chinese Buddhist activities.

China is clever. When a new Buddhist institute was established in Katmandu in 1961, with King Mahendra of Nepal presiding and laying the cornerstone, the Chinese Buddhist Association presented the institute with 500,000 rupees, and found as a result that many people were able to forget the experience of Tibet. In many countries, China has organized exhibitions of Touen Houang art, a form of Buddhist art found in the 486 caves of Touen Houang and dating back to the period from the fifth to the fourteenth centuries. The exhibitions of this art at the museum in Tokyo in 1958 and in Colombo in 1960 were very successful. The impression by Buddhists of other countries is that China pays a great deal of attention to the art and literature of Buddhism, since they see not only reproductions of these paintings but beautifully printed volumes concerning them, all produced at the national publishing house in Peking.

One of the cleverest things China did was to send a team with a

Buddhist relic, reported to be a tooth of the Lord Buddha, to other countries so that the Buddhists there might see and worship. This relic was brought from Udyanna to China at the end of the fifth century by a Buddhist monk named Fa-hsien. In 1955 a delegation of Buddhist clergy brought this relic to Burma, and wherever it was exhibited great crowds gathered to see and worship. The influence it had on the population was, of course, very great. The exhibition of the relic in Ceylon in 1961 had similar effects. A Buddhist delegation from Ceylon to Peking on May 28, 1961, was greeted by Chou En-lai, the foreign minister, himself, and arrangements to hand over the relic were managed with great skill and impressiveness.

Communist China would like to use the sympathies of the Buddhists as part of her means of opposing the West, since she is aware that there is a strong tendency in Buddhism to identify Western imperialism with Christianity. Both in their way of living and in their political thinking, Christians in Asia frequently identify more with Western attitudes than with those of their own community. Moreover, they have often relied heavily on the power and authority of the Western nations, and have shown a tendency to despise the culture and the traditions of their own people, including Buddhism.

The Chinese authorities seem also to have explored the possibilities of exploiting the close relationship of Buddhism and nationalism in their opposition to the West. Indeed, it is only the Chinese Communist ideology that stands in the way of the complete support by the Buddhists of all Southeast Asia for China in her contest with the West. But the past fifteen years have seen also the development of an anti-Communist tendency within Buddhism, and this has led Buddhists throughout Asia to resist all efforts that would make Buddhism the tool of Communist ideology.

MODERN REVIVAL OF BUDDHISM IN VIETNAM

In Vietnam, the revival of Buddhism started in the 1930's. By then, the patriotic resistance movement had become so strong that the French had to resort to all kinds of measures to curb it. About this time, under the impact of the movement for the renovation of Buddhism in China led by the great Chinese monk Tai Hsu, a number of Buddhists tried to start a parallel renewal movement in Vietnam. The French were aware of this, and authorized the establishment of a great many Buddhist associations in the three parts of the country. Moreover, the French even went so far as to lend official sponsorship to these associations. Their reasoning was very simple: instead of leaving the initiative of establishing their own associations to the natives, who might then use them against the administration, the government would take them over, install its own men among the ranks, and thus control them. Furthermore, this magnanimous religious policy would win the gratitude and good will of the Vietnamese. Another great advantage of this clever policy was that the people would then be occupied with religious observances and thus be distracted from patriotic agitation.

Among the many new religious organizations so established only a few were of importance, namely the Cochinchina Buddhist Study Society (Hoi Nam Ky Nghien Cuu Phat Hoc), the Luong Xuyen Buddhist Study Society (Luong Xuyen Phat Hoc Hoi), the Annam Buddhist Study Society (An Nam Phat Hoc Hoi), and the Vietnam Buddhist Association (Hoi Viet Nam Phat Giao). Each of these organizations had its own publication, its own license and charter.

Let us examine briefly one of these: the Cochinchina Buddhist Study Society. Its constitution was approved on August 26, 1931, and it had a periodical of its own, *Tu Bi Am* (*The Compassionate Voice*). The first issue carried the pictures of M. Khrautheimer, governor-general of Cochinchina, and M. Rivoal, mayor of Saigon, respectively honorary president and vice-president of the society. This issue also published government communiqué No. 129, regarding the status of the monks and the governor-general's intervention in connection with land that had been taken illegally from the Buddhist pagodas. The publication said that the intervention was a favor granted by the government, since the abbots of Buddhist pagodas had no right to own land. It was obvious that the founders of the society had close connections with the colonial authorities and were very proud of this great service rendered to Buddhism.

Gradually, however, the Buddhist study societies succeeded in infusing real life into the Buddhist movement, throughout the country. A number of dedicated Buddhists joined these societies and used their wisdom and talents to turn them into genuine associations for the study and practice of Buddhism. These associations contributed importantly to the renovation of the native culture, the reformation of Buddhism, the abolition of superstitions, and gradually gave Buddhism intellectual prestige. Many monasteries and Buddhist institutes were reopened, and the idea of the role of Buddhism in the future society of Vietnam gradually took shape. In the 1930's, the Buddhist scholars had already discussed the engagement of Buddhism in the modern society and called it Nhan Gian Phat Giao, or engaged Buddhism.[22]

Nevertheless, the movement for the renovation of Buddhism was solidly based only when the Buddhist institutes became established in all three parts of Vietnam.[23] In addition, a number of monks were sent abroad to China, Thailand, and Japan for their studies and, from 1950 on, others were sent to India, Ceylon, and the West. The year 1940 witnessed the birth of the first unit of the Buddhist youth movement (Thanh Nien Phat Hoc Duc Duc), under the guidance of Minh Tam Le Dinh Tham, a lecturer at Tay Thien Buddhist Institute. The members of this unit were given thorough instruction in Buddhism and entrusted with the care of the periodical *Vien Am* and with the formation of the Gia Dinh Phat Hoa Pho, later renamed Gia Dinh Phat Tu, or Buddhist Youth Family, a nationwide Buddhist youth organization. Under the direction of the Doan Thanh Nien Phat Hoc Duc Duc, the periodical *Vien Am* became a youthful and dynamic publication. The Buddha's teachings were presented in a new light by a young generation of Western-educated intellectuals, and this helped enormously in the task of bringing Buddhism to the young.

The Buddhist Youth Family movement has become one of the best-organized youth associations in the entire country. In parallel fashion to the country's scout and guide movement, it has its own ideals and methods of youth education. In 1962, South Vietnam alone could count as many as 1,000 units of this movement, comprising 70,000 active young people under the guidance of 3,000

[22] Among the promoters of this school, we notice Do Nam Tu and Thien Chieu, who fostered it in the bimonthly *Duoc Tue* (*Torch of Wisdom*), published in Hanoi. The idea of "National Buddhism" became fully developed when the *Vietnam Phat Dien Tung San* (collection of Vietnamese Buddhist literature) was published by the Vietnam Buddhist Association in conjunction with the Far Eastern Archeological School (Ecole Française d'Extrême Orient) in Hanoi, and when the Venerable Thich Mat The published the first work on the history of Vietnamese Buddhism (*Viet Nam Phat Giao Su Luoc,* Tan Viet, 1942) ever to be written in Vietnamese.

[23] The most widely known among these institutes are the Tay Thien, the Kim Son, the Bao Quoc, the Luong Xuyen, and the Lien Hai institutes.

leaders. The growth of this youth movement led to the opening of the Bodhi (Bo-De) primary and high schools in the provinces. These schools administer government-planned education and are managed by the local Buddhist organizations. At present, every province has its Bodhi schools. In addition there are many other private schools under Buddhist management that do not have the appellation Bodhi, such as Van Hanh, Ham Long, Tue Quang, Hong Lac, etc.

In the field of social welfare, Buddhist orphanages, nursery schools, and hospitals have been established throughout the country. In addition literacy campaigns and first-aid courses have also been organized everywhere. The nuns, who used to remain inactive in the monasteries, have been assigned to such institutions as hospitals, nurseries, and schools.

In 1945 the revolution broke out and led to the assumption of power by the Viet Minh. This great change in the political setup had an important impact on religious activities. While everyone was invited to join such new organizations as Youth to Save the Fatherland, Women's Association to Save the Fatherland, Catholics to Save the Fatherland, Buddhists to Save the Fatherland, etc., the young and responsible Buddhists managed to direct their time and efforts toward the modernization of Buddhism. They published a paper for youth named *Giai Thoat (Liberation)*, with the purpose "of studying Buddhism and applying it to modern life." This publication reflected the Buddhists' desire to transform their traditional religion to conform to the way of life of a society that aspired to revolutionary change. The publication also mirrored the frustration and doubts of the Buddhists who were witnessing the divisions and mutual liquidation of the political parties that had taken an active part in the revolution. Vo Dinh Cuong's novel (*Nhung Cap Kinh Mau (The Colored Eyeglasses)*, written at this time, also reflects the state of conflict and grave disagreement. The Buddhist intellectuals were now realizing the position of Buddhism in a new political orientation.

On December 27, 1946, the French fleet attacked Haiphong and opened the way for the return of the French troops to Vietnam. The Indochina war broke out and Emperor Bao Dai came back to Vietnam and resumed power. This war lasted until 1954, when Vietnam was "partitioned" after the Geneva Conference.

Right after the Indochina war started, a number of Buddhists began to publish the periodical *Giac-Ngo (Enlightenment)* at Hue in order to spread their doctrine of combined nationalism and humanism. The year 1950 saw the birth of a new Buddhist association in South Vietnam, under the guidance of a Buddhist scholar, Mai Tho Truyen.

On May 6, 1951, a national congress was held at Hue with the view of unifying the Buddhist associations of the country. The congress was attended by six important Buddhist communities of southern, central, and northern Vietnam.[24] At the conclusion of the congress, delegates from the three parts of Vietnam issued a declaration on the unification of their organizations and announced the establishment of the Tong Hoi Phat Grao, All-Vietnam Buddhist Association.

Later this new body published an official periodical called *Phat Giao Viet Nam* (*Vietnamese Buddhism*),[25] which clarified the nationalist and humanist line of Vietnamese Buddhism. An editorial in *Vietnamese Buddhism* reads:

Vietnamese Buddhism is not merely a religious belief that limits itself, everywhere and at all times, to its mission as a faith. On the contrary, everywhere it spreads, Buddhism adapts itself to the customs, cultural climate, and human elements of the land, influencing the local population's way of life. This is also true of Vietnam, where Buddhism has blended with and assimilated our national characteristics and has made common cause with the people in building an independent national culture.

According to the glorious history of our people, the Vietnamese have always desired to create their independent culture in order to resist the oppressive threat from the north. In this great and noble task of creating a national culture Vietnamese Buddhism played an important part. This is proved by the great achievements of Buddhism under the dynasties of Dinh Le, Ly, and Tran. The truth is that Vietnamese Buddhism is a national religion.

[24] The Vietnamese Buddhist Association and the Vietnam Buddhist Sangha of Northern Vietnam, the Central Vietnam Buddhist Association and Central Vietnam Buddhist Sangha, the Southern Vietnam Buddhist Study Society and the Southern Vietnam Buddhist Sangha.

[25] In its first issue this publication carried an article on "The Achievements of Vietnamese Buddhism under the Ly and Tran Dynasties," these two dynasties being the golden era of Vietnamese Buddhism and nationhood. In another article, "The Vietnamese Buddhist's Direction," which appeared in the same issue, the author, Da Thao, maintained that the humanism of Buddhism differed from both communism and all fanatical religious beliefs.

In the mind and heart of the Vietnamese people there is already the seed of Buddhism. For nearly two thousand years, the destiny of the nation and Buddhism have been intertwined. Let us join hands in cultivating Buddhism in order to bring peace and happiness to our nation.

"To bring peace and happiness to our nation"—this longing for peace by the Buddhists of Vietnam was as ardent and real then as it is now.[26]

The idea of Buddhism as a national religion did not take shape in the 1940's but much earlier—in the days of the Truc Lam Zen sect on Mount Yen Tu. But the idea crystallized during the hardship and suffering that the Buddhists had to endure under the French occupation and the regime of President Ngo Dinh Diem. The campaign to overthrow the Ngo Dinh Diem regime in 1963 not only succeeded in mobilizing the people to the defense of Buddhism but also awakened the nationalistic consciousness of the masses. In every Buddhist the idea of Buddhism and nationalism are intertwined and cannot be easily separated. Many non-Buddhist elements also took part in the Buddhist campaign, not because they wanted to support the Buddhists but because they realized that the Buddhist campaign was consistent with the people's aspirations.

After the November 1, 1963, revolution, which overthrew the regime of President Ngo Dinh Diem, the prestige of Buddhism reached its apex and attracted many intellectuals, students, and youth. However, at this stage Buddhism was not yet prepared to respond fully to this enthusiastic support. Most of the monks had not been trained to shoulder Buddhism's new mission. They had been trained to recite the sutras, to meditate, and to preach, and now became embarrassed at the role of responsible leadership suddenly thrust upon them. The number of monks and laymen with sufficient ability and experience to exercise leadership was small, while the need for responsible leaders became pressing. The

---

[26] The publication *Phat Giao Viet Nam* contained many articles about Buddhism as a national religion. For instance, Minh Hanh's series of articles, entitled "Toward National Buddhism," dwelt long on many problems of Vietnamese Buddhism, such as Buddhist history, Buddhist doctrine, Buddhist rites and music, the problems of organization and propagation of the doctrine. The desire to update Buddhism became more and more pressing. This desire was obvious in such series of articles as "The Essentials of Buddhism" in Lien Hoa publication, Hue, and "The Buddha of Our Time" in Tu Quang, Saigon. The reaction against the personalist philosophy of the regime was also real and evident.

intellectuals, artists, writers, students, politicians, workers, trade union officers, and farmers who were inclined to support Buddhism were many but they lacked leadership. Throughout the French occupation, which lasted for nearly one hundred years, Buddhism did not have many opportunities to send its monks to study abroad, nor did it have any facilities to train social workers and cultural cadres. Those who later served in the Buddhist cultural and social institutions were mostly dedicated laymen who volunteered, rather than cadres trained by the Buddhist Church itself. Furthermore, the Church lacked the financial means to meet the considerable expense of sending a monk abroad to study.

A shortage of qualified men was therefore inevitable. The Buddhist leaders were forced to take on people of lesser ability, who claimed to be Buddhists but actually were not. Moreover, in 1964 and 1965, remnants of the former Can Lao party of Ngo Dinh Nhu resumed their accustomed activity and caused a great deal of difficulty for the new Unified Buddhist Church. The Church had to meet their sabotage, reprisals, and attempts to return to power, and this alone consumed much of its energy. In addition, there were opportunists who managed to slip into the entourage of the Church leaders and traffic with the influence of the Church. Their influence on the monks was to account for many of the latters' mistakes.

During this time, the responsible and capable elements of the Church brought all their thoughts and efforts to the task of updating Buddhism. In Saigon, the young monks established two publishing houses: Van Hanh and La Boi. They both made known their desire to "actualize" (hien dai hoa) Buddhism. In addition, the weeklies *Hai Trieu Am* (*The Roar of the Ocean Tide*), *Thien My* (*Good and Beauty*), *Duoc Tue* (*The Torch of Wisdom*), *Dai Tu Bi* (*The Great Compassion*) and the monthlies *Van Hanh* (name of a Zen monk), *Giu Thom Que Me* (*Preserving the Reputation of the Motherland*), *Lien Hoa* (*The Lotus*), *Tu Quant* (*The Light of Compassion*), all speak the language of modern Buddhism. Also, the Church implicitly gave its sponsorship to two dailies, *Chanh Dao* (*The Right Path*) and *Dat To* (*The Fatherland*). In 1964, Van Hanh University was founded in Saigon and is the first Buddhist university organized along Western lines. The university started with two faculties, in Buddhist studies and the Humanities. In his inauguration speech, the Rector Thich Tri Thu said:

The education that is needed for the present time is one that can wash away from the innocent minds of the young generation all the dogmatic knowledge that has been forced upon them with the purpose of turning them into mere tools of various ideologies and parties. Such a system of education will not only liberate us from the prison of dogma but will also teach us understanding, love, and trust. These qualities: understanding, love, and trust are the prescriptions needed for the revival of our society that has been paralyzed by suspicion, intrigue, hatred, and frustration.

Buddhist study will not carry the students far in the race for position and wealth. The history of the Tran Dynasty has amply proved this. But the intellectuals of that time had to bear a heavy responsibility for the nation's history when they abandoned Buddhist education for the Confucian system, which was but a preparation for degrees and careers. In the firm belief in the resourcefulness of our nation I wish and desire that we could revive the lively spirit of the educational system of the Ly and Tran Dynasties with a view to freeing our minds and kindling again love and trust in order to save our nation.

The Buddhists of Vietnam desire to mobilize the potential force of their religion in order to rebuild their society, and consequently they have carried Buddhism into every domain of life: culture, economics, politics, and social welfare. Such a revolutionary effort naturally requires time for its realization. In the process, the Buddhist leaders have made mistakes because they have had to face new difficulties arising from the outside and at the same time to solve internal crises that inevitably accompany any radical change.

Many outsiders tend to regard as useless and harmful to the country the contemporary agitations that are connected with the Buddhist Church. This judgment is far too simple. These upheavals must be accepted with the pains that necessarily accompany the current revolution in Vietnamese society. They are the necessary disorders which naturally attend the development of a nation to maturity. If we fail to see these simple things, we may come to believe the widely propagated calumny that Vietnamese Buddhism is not a force in itself but is a mere tool of the Communists or the National Liberation Front. In fact, anyone with some elementary knowledge of the growth of the movement for the modernization of Vietnamese Buddhism must see that Buddhism is a great spiritual force in search of self-realization amid the chaotic disorders of a society in its utmost stage of disintegration because of the war and political intrigue.

The desire of the Buddhists to reconstruct their country from the grass roots up is materializing through the establishment in Saigon of a community development school whose aims are to train rural development cadres and to mobilize the latent resources of Buddhism to carry out the task of developing the rural areas. This is the self-appointed task of the School of Youth for Social Service of Van Hanh University. This institution aims to train young people who are willing to work for the improvement and development of the rural areas. It maintains that democracy has its chance only in fairly developed societies.

In the case of Vietnam, industrialization depends largely on rural development. The programs of the school are not mere relief operations but are aimed at radically rebuilding the rural communities. For a long time there has existed a very wide gap between the Vietnamese rural population and the intellectuals. Many of the latter have studied abroad and brought back impressive diplomas but cannot fully understand and befriend the rural masses who constitute up to 90 per cent of the national population. The intellectuals' training and way of living do not enable them to meet the needs of the rural communities. One of the objectives of the School of Youth for Social Service is to raise up a new generation of youth who can mix with the villagers, befriend them, and use the rural-development skills to guide the villagers in co-operative community-development projects. In 1964, some experimental voluntary villages were established, to which the school has recently added a number of pilot villages.

To assist in the instruction of the population in Buddhism, a national preachers' college consisting of many capable monks was organized as early as 1951. However, this has not been able to meet the demands of the immense Buddhist population in the country. Since 1951, the demand of the Buddhist youth movement for chaplains has increased manifold until, in 1964, the Church was unable to provide enough chaplains for the various associations of students, scouts, guides, and particularly for the armed forces. Despite this shortage, the training of preachers has progressed rather slowly because the number of available monks is limited and training facilities remain inadequate.

As is common to any church organization, both conservative and progressive elements are present in the Buddhist Church. The former are slow to respond to the need for actualizing Buddhism, while the latter desire to speed up the reorganization of the Church in order to take a more active part in the life of the society. The young monks belong to the latter element, grouped as they are about the Church's cultural and social institutions but lacking key positions in the Church itself. The influence of their thought and action is strong among the population, however. They have a greater awareness of the issues that Vietnam has to face, in economics, culture, education, and social welfare, and are anxious to make use of the potential resources of Buddhism in order to solve these problems. The young monks naturally have the support of the intellectuals and younger generation. However, this support is not the Church's support. Conservative dogmatism and fear of change have always hindered progress. The real issue is how the Buddhist Church can get on with its internal revolution while fulfilling its duty toward society.

III. THE STRUGGLE TODAY

Enter Communism

REVOLUTION AND INTRIGUES

IN 1945, when Ho Chi Minh took power, the Vietnamese people, except for a small group of intellectuals and religious leaders, knew nothing of communism or its nature. Under Ho Chi Minh there came to power many of those who had opposed the French but had had to seek refuge in China or had been trained in the Soviet Union, and had been therefore well trained in Communist approach. Among the ablest of these were Pham Van Dong, now Premier of North Vietnam; Dang Xuan Khu (alias Truong Chinh), now President of the Assembly in North Vietnam; Vo Nguyen Giap, Minister of Defense; Dang Thai Mai, Hoang Minh Giam, Tran Huy Lieu, and Ho Tung Mau. Within a period of three or four months Trotskyites and non-Communists were eliminated from posts in government, including such leaders as Ta Thu Thau, Ho Van Nga, Bui Quang Chieu, and Pham Quynh. Mr. Tran Huy Lieu, Minister for Propaganda, actively promoted the doctrines of communism.

Opposition by the non-Communist nationalist forces became stronger, however, with the return to Vietnam of hundreds of exiled leaders, and with the arrival in Vietnam of 180,000 Kuo Min Tang Chinese troops, sent to disarm the Japanese. Among these nationalist leaders were Nguyen Hai Than, Vu Hong Khanh, and Nguyen Tuong Tam. The last-named of these, one of Vietnam's most respected writers who subsequently abandoned his political career in order to concentrate on writing, committed suicide during the Diem regime when he was called to trial by Diem. Saying that he would not be judged by the Diem government, but only by history, he took his life in protest against the repressions of what he considered to be a profoundly unjust government.

Protected by Siao Wen, political adviser to General Lu Han, who commanded the Chinese forces, these nationalists opened a front to oppose the Hanoi regime and to insist on a coalition government of Communists and non-Communists. Their activities were supported by many Vietnamese who were aware of the nature of communism. Searching for means to resolve this problem, Ho Chi Minh, in November, 1945, dissolved the North Indo-Chinese Communist party and proposed a Vietnam-wide election. Leaders of the Vietnamese Nationalist parties Dai Viet, Dong Minh Hoi, and Viet Nam Quoc Dan Dang (Vietnamese Kuo Min Tang) were unwilling to accept this proposal, however, maintaining that they should be immediately incorporated in a coalition government. They created a coalition front of allied nationalists, and published the journal *Thiet Thuc* as a means of anti-government propaganda.

On December 12, at a ceremony commemorating Sun Yat-sen, Nguyen Hai Than, of the Dong Minh Hoi, organized a big meeting in Hanoi in a demonstration against the Ho Chi Minh government. The meeting turned into a riot between Communists and nationalists. Siao Wen, the Chinese political adviser, intervened with a proposal for a united national government in order to achieve the strength to oppose the French attempt to reconquer South Vietnam. Ho Chi Minh agreed, but said that the government could not be formed until after the elections had taken place, which he said could happen within a few weeks. Again the Nationalist Front refused to agree, and kidnapped Vo Nguyen Giap and Tran Huy Lieu. As in the present situation in Vietnam, they feared that given a few weeks of preparation, the government could so influence the elections or suppress their forces that their chances would be eliminated.

The Nationalist coalition failed and soon collapsed. Its failure came about for several reasons. Most of the Vietnamese did not understand the struggle that was going on, since they knew very little about communism and were not really aware of the way in which the Communists had dominated the Ho Chi Minh government. They were angry at the support that the Nationalists had from the Chinese troops, who were resented as outsiders and whose rude and arrogant conduct alienated the people. Finally, none of the Nationalist parties had constructed a positive political or ideological program, and could oppose the Communists by no more than vague appeals to nationalism and non-communism.

HO CHI MINH, A NATIONAL HERO

During this period there was very little popular understanding or even consciousness of the difference between Communist and non-Communist approaches to independence. What excited the people were the concepts of patriotism and national independence, and these brought a whole new vitality throbbing through the life of Vietnam in the years immediately after the revolution of 1945. All kinds of organizations were created to capitalize on this sense of excitement, and to channel the people's energies: Youth to Save the Fatherland, Women's Association to Save the Fatherland, Older People's Associations to Save the Fatherland, and so on. Almost no one was exempted, and the people's enthusiasm for the revolution was such that they joined these groups willingly. Even religious communities established their own groups: Catholics to Save the Fatherland, Buddhists to Save the Fatherland, etc.

All of this was helped, and the opposition to communism weakened, by the attempt of the French in the South to re-establish their rule over Vietnam. It was that attempt, which was to be supported and largely financed by the United States, that consolidated the people's support behind the Hanoi government and made the victory of communism in North Vietnam certain. In the minds of the Vietnamese people in general, Ho Chi Minh was a national hero who had led their struggle against the French. Except for a very small group of intellectuals, no one thought of him as a Communist, or as one who was about to establish a Communist regime in Vietnam.

The French returned in 1947, and the Indochinese War then continued until 1954. On the one side the French, supported by the United States, "co-operated" with a "Nationalist" government headed by the Emperor Bao Dai, who had renounced the throne in 1945 to become a Counselor to the Ho Chi Minh government, had subsequently left Vietnam first for Hong Kong and then for Europe, and then returned officially to Vietnam on April 24, 1949, under French auspices as "Chief of State." On the other side were the Viet Minh.

The Vietnamese naturally saw Bao Dai as a puppet of the French and gave him as little support as they gave to the French themselves. The people's hearts turned to the "chien Khu" (maquis) and to the resistance forces. Once again the resistance was formed of a united front of the Dan Chu (Democratic party), the Xa Hoi (Socialist party), the Lien Viet (the Vietnamese alliance), and the Ton Giao (the religious groups). This period gave the Communists an opportunity to expand their power very rapidly, and in March, 1951, the Communist Labor party (Lao Dong) was created, and became therefore the successor to the formerly disbanded Indo-Chinese Communist party. Dang Xuan Khu (Truong Chinh) became Secretary-General of the party.

The brutalities of the French continued to increase the hostility of the people. Innumerable young people left their studies in the cities to join the resistance movement in the fight against the hated invader. During this period the majority of the population continued to see the resistance as only a movement for national independence, and were unaware of the development of the Communist force within it. The so-called "Nationalist" government of Bao Dai did carry on extensive anti-Communist propaganda, but it was unsuccessful because the people did not believe anything said either by the French or by their puppet Chief of State. The Vietnamese assumed that everything that the Bao Dai government and the French did was directed against their own interests, and the anti-Communist propaganda of these groups therefore had exactly the opposite effect from what was intended. People cannot believe in the words of those who have invaded their homelands and are engaged in shooting, destroying, burning their homes, and terrorizing their fellow citizens, and this irrespective of the objective truth of what they may be saying. The Bao Dai government, seen entirely as a mindless puppet of the French, failed completely in its effort to create an anti-Communist awareness. The Communist forces, in the meantime, identified themselves completely with the patriotic struggle against the invaders, grew very rapidly, and developed for themselves a firm base on which to operate.

By the end of 1953 the Viet Minh were completely in control of three fourths of North Vietnam and a third of South Vietnam. On May 7, 1954, Dien Bien Phu fell, and the French were unable to continue their military effort. Two months later on July 21, 1954, the cease-fire agreements were signed at Geneva and Vietnam was "temporarily" divided along the seventeenth parallel.

The division, as most people know, was specifically not intended to be a permanent political boundary, but to serve only as a cease-fire line until free elections, under international supervision, could reunify the country in 1956. However, Ngo Dinh Diem, who be-

came premier of South Vietnam under Bao Dai while the Geneva
Conference was going on, and who subsequently, with strong
American support, deposed his chief and became president, re-
fused to permit these elections to be held.

Among those in the West who oppose the war in Vietnam, and
particularly the role of the United States in it, there are many who
attribute the outbreak of the fighting in the 1959-60 period, and
the creation of the Viet Cong, to this failure to have elections.
Had the elections been held, they say, the country would have
been peacefully united under its national hero, Ho Chi Minh, and
there would have been no guerrilla warfare. The elections were
not held, they maintain, because the results clearly would have
favored Ho Chi Minh's government, which would have meant
friendly relations with China and the Soviet Union and the exclu-
sion of the United States as the dominant power in South Vietnam.
Therefore the United States ordered its puppet Diem to refuse to
abide by the Geneva Agreements, and the victorious Viet Minh,
once again cheated at the conference table of a victory they had
won in battle, renewed the war.

The facts are not quite so simple. Certainly the refusal to hold
the elections was a clear violation of the Geneva Agreements and
was a considerable factor in making the renewed war possible.
But it is very doubtful that the war could have been resumed, or
its resumption been successful, if Diem had been able to create in
South Vietnam a legitimately democratic, non-Communist government with a record of genuine social reform to its credit.

For many Vietnamese it is true that Ho Chi Minh was a national
hero. But for others, including many of the most devoted nationalist leaders who had fought through the whole struggle against the
French, there were vivid memories of the ruthlessness with which
Ho's Communist apparatus had liquidated his non-Communist
allies as soon as the war had ended, both in 1945 and 1954. Among
these leaders, already defeated in two sharp struggles with the Ho
Communists in an effort to build a genuine coalition government
for their country, there was little enthusiasm for a unified country
under Ho. Many of them would have welcomed the opportunity to
build a strong non-Communist democratic government in South
Vietnam, since that would have given them exactly what they had
been looking for since 1945: a base from which it would have
been possible to negotiate a coalition agreement with the Com-

munist North Vietnamese in which their own interests and democratic principles would have been safeguarded.

It was because Diem did not do this, but instead instituted a
bitterly repressive regime of his own, harshly liquidated the very
groups and individuals that might have helped him, and condoned
or instigated forms of social injustice, that the Viet Cong could
attract support and launch a formidable attack on his regime.

NGO DINH DIEM, A CATHOLIC DICTATOR

From 1955 on, the United States began to send in "advisers" to
work with the Diem government on technical, political, and military matters. A referendum arranged by the Diem government in
October, 1955, resulted in the overthrow of Bao Dai and the election of Diem as president of South Vietnam.

With the assistance of the United States, President Ngo Dinh
Diem was able to demonstrate his anti-French attitudes, although
of course these came after the French had been defeated at Dien
Bien Phu. The alleged efforts of the Diem government to resume
sovereignty from the French presented no difficulties whatever,
given American help, but added prestige to the Diem reputation.
The Vietnamese, who had hated the French colonialists for a
long time, now welcomed anyone who could demonstrate himself
to be anti-French. In September, 1954, Diem had dissolved the
joint Franco-Vietnamese tribunals and the French-dominated fed-
eral security police. He also ended French domination of financial
matters by terminating French control of the Indo-Chinese bank
in favor of the establishment of a national bank and a national
bureau of exchange. The agreement signed with the French on
December 29, 1954, acknowledged the right of the Vietnamese to
control their own foreign trade. The administration of Saigon
University was transferred from French control to the Vietnamese
government. Beginning with Diem's accession to the Premiership
in July, 1954, American aid was channeled directly to the Vietnamese instead of through the French. Norodom Palace, which
had been referred to as the palace of the Governor-General, was
turned over to the Vietnamese and was renamed "dinh doc lap"
(Independence Palace). The ceremony of the transfer of Norodom
Palace was emphasized as symbolic of the resumption of Vietnamese sovereignty after a century of domination by the French.

At the time, the United States had no combat troops in Vietnam, and the relationship between American policy and French policy was unknown to the Vietnamese. Furthermore, people in the cities especially were able to observe the help that the Americans were giving in the solution of economic and social problems, and consequently did not look on them with the hostility they had had for the French. It was the most favorable period for Americans in Vietnam; it is unfortunate that they did not make better use of it.

President Diem's most valuable contribution was the awareness that he created of a distinction between national resistance and Communists.[27]

[27] Because "anti-communism" has taken on a mystical, nonrational, almost religious character in the United States and some other Western countries, I want to explain that I do not use it in these terms in referring to my own attitude or that of Vietnamese Buddhist or other nationalist leaders.

Communism has a base of social and personal idealism, and recruits thousands of men and women who are passionately concerned to eliminate the exploitation and inequality that have characterized much of Western society, and to create a form of social organization whose slogan will be "from each according to his ability, to each according to his need." This is an objective which is theoretically consistent with the best in most of the world's great religions, and with which religious men can have no quarrel.

Moreover, the economic organization of society in socialist terms, meaning a society in which the means of production are operated for the good of the people generally rather than for the profit of a minority, is consistent with the needs of a country like Vietnam. Few Vietnamese Buddhist or nationalist leaders could believe that their country could afford a Western-type capitalism, even if they thought it was a moral form of social organization.

Vietnamese anti-communism stems from the methods that organized communism uses to attain its ends: the suppression of all significant dissent and debate; the liquidation of even the most sincere and committed opponents, violently if need be; the assumption of omniscience on the part of the party, which is a form of fanaticism that is stultifying to a never-ending search for truth—to which Buddhists, for example, are committed; and the willingness to sacrifice the very existence of a small country like Vietnam to the "larger" interests of the Communist side in the cold war between the great powers. This is not theorizing for Vietnamese non-Communist nationalists, who have found themselves and their organizations repressed with the same ruthlessness north and south of the 17th parallel, by the North Vietnamese-NLF-China coalition as well as by the Diem-Ky-U.S. grouping.

I do not mean to imply that all Vietnamese nationalists who are also anti-Communist share exactly the same view. Some of them undoubtedly are far to the right, politically. Many would oppose the Communist tactics on the quite simple grounds that they believe in their own goals for Vietnam and want to work for them. For many of us, however, for whom the

In the cities especially, the intellectuals and small bourgeoisie began to understand and support the anti-Communist policies of the Diem government. It was the whole aura surrounding the regime's resumption of Vietnamese sovereignty that made it possible for it to accomplish this. Many of the Diem projects were well-conceived in themselves and could have been valuable, but the government became increasingly corrupt and inefficient through Diem's desire to control everything himself, and through his failure to enlist the help of talented non-Communist nationalists in his government. From the moment of his assumption of power, Diem spared no effort to eliminate every form of opposition to his regime, and had no faith in anyone except members of his own family and of his own church. With a few talented exceptions, the coterie who surrounded him were incompetent sycophants, seeking to re-enforce their own positions by leaning on the government and the Church.

Various groups in South Vietnam at this time sought to participate in the government in the hope of making it a genuinely representative one. Such groups as the Cao Dai and the Hoa Hao, who had their own armies and controlled certain areas of Vietnam, used these as a base from which to seek participation in government. However Diem and his American advisers chose instead to suppress all of these groups forcibly, maintaining that a state could not exist within a state. The Diem government became obsessed with the problem of eliminating all opposition, but gave no thought to the consolidation of the various non-Communist forces in South Vietnam. Diem put his entire reliance on violent suppression instead of resorting to more humanistic political means of consolidating the state's existence.

Pro-French military leaders, including Nguyen Van Hinh and Nguyen Van Vy, were ousted from participation in government. On the other hand, non-Communist nationalist forces, which had been part of the joint struggle against the French, were also liquidated by Diem, including the Binh Xuyen in Saigon province and the surrounding areas; the Cao Dai in Tay Ninh province and other provinces in South and central Vietnam; the Hoa Hao in

---

stated objectives of communism are largely acceptable, the opposition we feel grows from our conviction that when such methods are used to attain these "good" ends, the ends themselves become unattainable because the methods used corrupt the whole struggle. If humanistic religion has any meaning at all, it is that humanistic ends cannot be achieved by inhuman and depersonalizing means.

a number of provinces in South Vietnam; the Dai Viet in Quang Tri, Thua Thien, and Phu Yen provinces; and the Quoc Dan Dang in Quang Nam, Quang Ngai, and Binh Dinh provinces. Some of these secretly sought help from the French, whose troops were still there, in the effort to maintain their power.

President Ngo Dinh Diem was himself a Catholic, but he inherited much of the attitudes and spirit of the mandarins, since he came from a mandarin Confucian family that had occupied high positions under the Emperor Bao Dai. He used his power like a mandarin, operating as though he were a high governor or a king, even though the external structure of the society was that of a republic. He wanted to restore the spirit of *Trung* (fidelity) and *Nghia* (loyalty). These principles of Confucianism he attempted to introduce into the life of Vietnam as a means of strengthening his power. Again, his formal Catholicism was subordinate to his tendencies to behave as a mandarin, which in Chinese means the man who is "mother and father to the population." He sought and expected from the Vietnamese complete obedience and fidelity. Curiously enough, for a high minister who had deposed his sovereign Bao Dai, he spoke unceasingly of things like fidelity of subjects to rulers.

The Buddhists became aware very early that the regime of Ngo Dinh Diem was one under which they could not breathe easily. Kao Tan Nguyen, a Buddhist layman, in the magazine *Phat Giao Viet Nam,* the official bulletin of all Buddhist associations, attacked the policy of using feudal morality in order to build up the power of President Diem. The protest was in the form of a comedy describing a session of a tribunal being held in the nether world where politicians are tried.

The part of Ngo Dinh Diem is symbolized by the character of Ho Quy Ly, a Vietnamese politician of centuries ago. The attempt of Ngo Dinh Diem to use this feudal concept to strengthen his rule is related to the commentaries by Ho Quy Ly on the Four Books of Confucianism. In the play Ho Quy Ly is condemned as "bat trung" (lacking in fidelity); "bat nhan" (lacking in humaneness); "bat tri" (lacking in wisdom); and "bat nghia" (lacking in loyalty).

THE JUDGE: You are accused of having taken over the throne of another and of being therefore guilty of grand larceny. The effect of your robbery has been to divide the people, creating internal troubles and inviting external invasion. You have been accused of sowing all these troubles for your fellow human beings; now you have a chance to defend yourself.

HO QUY LY: It is not true that I have stolen the country. The royal court, according (*looking up*) to the will of God and (*looking down*) to the will of the people, put me on the throne in order to replace the Le Dynasty. I did not want it. It was not my intention—it was not my intention. It was something that I did with the greatest unwillingness. The country belongs to the whole population, and it was the whole population who lifted me up. The country does not belong to a single dynasty, and it is not right to say that I took it from them. The trouble is that Confucianism has become moribund, and it was not possible to distinguish right from wrong. That is why the *term* is not *right;* that is why the *speech* is turned upside down. That is why it has been necessary for me to write new commentaries on the Four Books of Confucianism as they were interpreted by the scholars Trinh and Chu. (*Pause.*) Your excellency, have you read my commentaries? If not, I promise to bring you copies so that you may see them.

THE JUDGE (*shouting*): Stop it! Stop that story! If you had no conspiracy, why did you build the western capital? Why do you force the people to exchange their gold and silver money for your paper money?

HO QUY LY: Yes, yes, of course. The things you mention reflect my "wisdom"! I suggest that you read my commentaries on the Four Books first and judge me later if you do not wish to commit any injustice.

THE JUDGE: There is nothing unjust here. You have taken the mandate from the King of Le, and you betrayed the Le Dynasty. This is something that a learned gentleman of Confucianism never, never does. You pretend to be one who can comment on the Four Books, a man who wants to continue the career of the sages, yet how can you do such a thing? If the king is incapable, you should not serve under him. Serving under an incapable king indicates a lack of wisdom. If you have served under an incapable king and then betrayed him, that is lack of loyalty and lack of fidelity. If the Court is bad, then you should not participate in it; if you participate in it, you do not turn your spear on your own associates. If you turn the spear on them, then you demonstrate a lack of humaneness and a lack of trustworthiness. Where there are so many "lacks," there is nothing to be gained by commenting on the Four Books, no matter how valuable the commentaries may be in themselves. Do you not know that if you are truly a hero, you build your career with your own horse and sword, on the basis of the doctrine, not by betraying others? [28]

At the time that this was published, I was editor of the magazine, and was entirely aware of the fact that if Kao Tan Nguyen had not written this disguised as a comedy, the magazine would have been censored and I would have been imprisoned.

The Americans were unaware of all of these developments that were certainly going to lead to the overthrow of President Diem. Instead of responding to the pressures for reform of the government that were coming from many groups within the Vietnamese society, the government concentrated still more on the liquidation of the various forms of opposition, violently and by devious methods. Even for those in the Cao Dai and the Hoa Hao who were prepared to end their resistance and co-operate, President Diem had prepared a trick. The Cao Dai general, Nguyen Thanh Phuong, for example, returned to the army, but was subsequently murdered by being shot in the back. And the Hoa Haoist leader, Le Quang Vinh (alias Ba Cut), was arrested when he came to discuss terms of co-operation and was subsequently executed.

All of these measures eroded the respect of the population for the regime, and the process continued as the regime slipped farther into nepotism and the manipulation of the Catholic Church for its own ends, and permitted the ambitious and opportunistic elements within the Church to use the government for their own advancement and the removal of their opposition. If the government had not committed these mistakes, but had created a genuinely democratic regime composed of the non-Communist elements within South Vietnam, it would have contributed greatly to the development of a stable society there. But the seeds of anger and distrust had been sown, and there was no real loyalty to the regime or belief in its pretensions. When the war broke out again, it seemed to most of the Vietnamese peasants to be a renewal of the war of resistance against the Western imperialists and their puppets, and not a war created by Communists bent on taking over their country. People so disillusioned and hurt were ripe for the propaganda of the new resistance movement, and in increasing numbers accepted

[28] The review *Phat Giao Viet Nam,* No. 9, Wesak (anniversary of the birth of the Buddha), 1956.

the interpretation of the American support of Ngo Dinh Diem as being an indication of American desire to establish a new kind of colonialism in their country.

THE NATIONAL LIBERATION FRONT

The refusal of Saigon to confer with Hanoi for general elections to reunify the country according to the 1954 Geneva Agreement became the reason for the shift of North Vietnam to an aggressive role. This shift on the part of Hanoi to the offensive occurred during 1958 and 1959. In South Vietnam, the National Liberation Front was created on December 20, 1960, in an attempt to ally all the forces of opposition against President Diem. Understandably, the NLF quickly got the support of North Vietnam. During the third convention of the North Vietnamese Labor (Communist) party, the general secretary, Le Duan, announced the creation of the NLF, and claimed that the Front was being led by the Party with the aim of overthrowing the Diem regime, revoking the South Vietnamese constitution, and realizing the unification of North and South.

It is common knowledge that there are very many patriotic, non-Communist elements in the National Liberation Front. They joined the Front because they agreed with it that they must oppose the regime of President Diem and the policies of the Americans, which they had begun to see as very similar to the earlier French policies. This was especially true when the extensive financial help that had been given to the French by the Americans during that earlier war became generally known. Since the United States supported the dictatorial Diem regime, it was itself identified with it by the Vietnamese people. They were increasingly convinced that the Americans were not in Vietnam to protect the freedom and democracy of the Vietnamese, but to defend their own national self-interests and the interests of the so-called "free world."

The Front could never have grown strong if the Diem regime had known how to deal with the non-Communist elements in Vietnam. The Diem regime succeeded in paralyzing most of the non-Communist elements who sought a democratic society; those that were not forced into immobility had no place to turn except to the Front. Thus the irony of history was that the very intensity of the Diem efforts to eliminate all forms of non-Communist opposition served eventually to assure the strengthening of the Front and the consequent strengthening of its Communist leadership. There were many brave and devoted South Vietnamese who spoke their minds, but they were subject to such persecution, arrest, and exile that they had no alternative but to flee. Unhappily, there was no place to flee except to the one effective center of opposition, the Front. The terrorism and suppression of the government toward these opponents greatly helped the Front to grow, both in numbers and in influence.

According to the documents of the Association for Political Research in Paris, there are at least four actual leaders of the Front whose names do not appear on its Central Committee but who are members of the Central Committee of the North Vietnamese Labor party. It is for this reason that it is safe to say that the Communists are at the center of the control mechanism of the Front. But the Central Leadership Committee of the Front has not been composed of Communists, and the population knows only the names of the official leadership. The majority of the people of the countryside, therefore, do not think of the Front as a Communist movement, but as a genuine movement for national liberation. The Front does not propagate Communist ideology; the Front talks only about liberation from the "American imperialists," and it is this that accounts for the great success of the Front. The majority of the Vietnamese people love their country, speak the same language as the members of the Front, and hate the foreigners who try to invade their country and control it, and so they are ready to listen to the propaganda of the Front and to believe that the Americans are in fact such invaders. They all believe that the purpose of the American presence in Vietnam today is to secure permanent military bases. That alone is enough to upset the people very much, but then there is added to it the growing domination of the economic, political, and social life of the country by American power and wealth.

In 1961, President Kennedy began to send over more military trainers, and the war took on a new aspect. American "advisers" began to operate directly with the South Vietnamese army, and from that time on the Vietnamese peasants looked on the Americans exactly in the way that they had looked on the French in an earlier time. Under the impact of the propaganda of the Front, the Diem government began to look more and more like the same kind of puppet that the Bao Dai government had been under the French, trying to realize the objectives of Western policy.

In January, 1962, there was created within the Front the Nhan Dan Cach Mang party, which, translated, is The People's Revolutionary party, and it was in fact the Communist Party of South Vietnam. It is accurate to say that it was therefore the South Vietnamese wing of the North Vietnamese Labor party. The creation of this party demonstrated the increasing importance of the Communists within the Front. The daily newspaper, *Nhan Dan,* in Hanoi, on April 4, 1962, wrote: "The People's Revolutionary Party is a pioneering force in the front line during this revolutionary struggle." Hanoi began to mention South Vietnam as the front line of resistance against American invasion. (The expression used is "tuyen dau to quoc," whose literal translation is something like "front line of the fatherland." Historically, this concept has referred in Vietnam to the northern line between Vietnam and China, and it is most significant that the Vietnamese should now be talking about it as in the South opposed to the Americans.)

Enter the United States

AMERICAN SOLDIERS: HOW THE PEASANT SEES THEM

The business of war itself has been taken over almost completely by the American troops now, with the South Vietnamese army occupying a strictly subordinate role. Thus it is exactly as in the time of the war against the French. The Vietnamese army is fed, clothed, and armed from the American budget; its guns, bullets, and planes all come from America. In Vietnam people refer to gasoline as being typical of the American control; the army would be powerless without the use of American gasoline. Without gasoline every army activity would be cut off. The resistance movement of the dissident army units of Da Nang and Hue in May, 1966, could not continue because of a lack of gasoline, and without American gasoline the troops of General Ky could not have suppressed it. Thus everyone knows that the Vietnam policy is made by Americans and that everything that Vietnam does, the United States is responsible for.

The more American troops sent to Vietnam, the more the anti-American campaign led by the NLF becomes successful. Anger and hatred rise in the hearts of the peasants as they see their villages burned, their compatriots killed, their houses destroyed. Pictures showing NLF soldiers with arms tied, followed by American soldiers holding guns with bayonets, make people think of the Indo-china war between the French and the Viet Minh and cause pain even to the anti-Communist Vietnamese.

Vietnamese, even if they are anti-Communists, cannot despise Viet Cong soldiers although they can despise military men on their side, because the Viet Cong fight with much more courage than the government soldiers do. They are able to do so not be-cause they are willing to serve communism—the majority of them do not know what communism is, and those who do know, do not like it. If they fight bravely, if they are willing to sacrifice them-selves, it is because they believe that they are really fighting for national independence, to liberate the nation from "the invasion of imperialist Americans."

Even under French rule, the Vietnamese peasants did not see as many French troops as they see Americans now. Early in 1965, the number of American soldiers had already reached 200,000. Now it approaches 400,000. The country is full of American soldiers. And these military men do not have any background in the culture, folklore, and the way of living of the Vietnamese people. In their dealings with the Vietnamese, in talking with them, and during military operations, they cannot avoid making mistakes. Being alone in the remote countryside, they can commit unpopular acts and it is quite impossible to control the behavior of 400,000 American soldiers.

It would not be too shocking to learn that a Vietnamese soldier has stolen a chicken from a peasant, but if an American G.I. does the same thing, or if he violates a Vietnamese woman, this will greatly harm Washington's prestige. The people of the Front are always there in order to exploit such events for anti-American propaganda. And such regrettable actions often occur. Americans living in their own country may be shocked and angered when they learn of such things. Many of them find it impossible to be-lieve. In fact people would understand better if they shared the hard life of the soldiers, living all day sometimes in the mud or in the jungle full of mosquitoes and other insects, watched by death. These soldiers tend to regard moral values as unimportant, es-pecially when they think they are not fighting for a right cause but only being forced to fight. They hate those who have pushed them into the situation where they may die meaninglessly.

The majority of the peasants take little or no interest in the problems of communism or anti-communism. They are direct victims of the war, and consequently they welcome every effort in the direction of ending the war. Except for those who believe that they must support the Front in order to expel the American "aggressors," everyone hates the war itself. The more the war is escalated, the more they are its victims, since both sides threaten their lives and property. Since early 1964 I have frequented the remote villages of Vietnam, along with teams of young social workers, and it is from these visits that I interpret the mind of the peasant.

On New Year's of 1965 we went up the Thu Bon River by rowboat to bring help to several remote villages that had been stricken by floods. These villages, Son Thuan, Khuong Binh, and Ca Tang, were typical of the great suffering afflicting many Vietnamese villages of this sort. Houses and gardens have been destroyed, families have lost their sons, and women their husbands, and the stream of life itself has been almost totally disrupted by the war. On the way up we were stopped by both government and NLF forces for examination. Even for us, it was impossible to tell them apart. Buddhist clergymen and nuns were in the boats, wearing the symbols of their faith, and explained to both sides that they were bringing help to the villages. Neither side showed any signs of liking us, but finally they did let us go through.

Peasants in these villages hated both sides. The Viet Cong ordered them to dig caves as shelters from the possible bombing, while government troops warned them that if they dug caves, the Viet Cong would use them for resistance against the government. They were warned that if they refused to dig the caves, they would suffer the consequences from the Viet Cong, and they were warned by the government that if they did dig the caves they would be beaten by the government troops. We talked with some peasants who were preparing to take some of their products to the market by boat, and when we had established confidence between ourselves I asked them the question: "Whom would you follow: the government of South Vietnam or the National Liberation Front?"

They replied: "We do not follow either. We follow the one who can end the war and guarantee that we can live."

The peasants are not concerned about ideology: no one can frighten them with stories of the evils of communism. With their property already destroyed, they do not fear that the Communists will take their property. And if one speaks to them of freedom and democracy, they say, "Of what use is freedom and democracy if one is not alive to enjoy them?" So it is clear that the first problem of the Vietnamese peasant is a problem of life itself: how to survive in the midst of all the forces that threaten him; how to cling to life itself.

Americans see war through the eyes of newspaper correspondents, in terms of guerrilla soldiers and their own boys fighting bravely against desperate foes. Vietnamese see the war somewhat differently. They see it as I saw it in a small village, oxen drawing a simple peasant cart along the road. In the cart was a young Vietnamese woman holding her month-old baby in her arms, and with her mother beside her. The cart was piled high with their possessions. Out of the sky there descended a helicopter, its blades rattling and its motor roaring. The oxen were frightened and ran away, throwing the women and their possessions all over the road. If it had been a motion-picture scene, it might have seemed funny, but to them it did not. American soldiers descended from the helicopter and made it plain that they wanted the young woman to go with them. Both women implored the soldiers for mercy, but there was no mercy. The young woman handed the baby to her mother and let herself be pushed into the helicopter and carried away.

This is the face of war as the Vietnamese villager sees it, and as all the simple victims of all wars have seen it. There is nothing good to be said of this kind of thing under any circumstances, but the damage is multiplied a thousandfold when they are white soldiers in a land of non-white peoples. It is because precisely these things happen that the Americans can never conceivably win a military victory in Vietnam; it is because such things happen that the longer they stay the more Communists they create. And of course it should be noted that the Viet Cong, who are the American's "enemy," look exactly like the other Vietnamese who are their "friends," and whom they are allegedly protecting. The result is an undiscriminating attack, with massive firepower, on village after village, and sometimes even on units of their own allies, in a futile attempt to destroy the Viet Cong.

Recently American journalists have reported a growing concern among American commanders and government officials in Vietnam over the very high rate of casualties among civilians. There is nothing new about this. Precisely because of the kinds of things I have described above, the war has consistently seen more civilians killed than Viet Cong. Between 1961 and 1964, even modest estimates of the casualties indicated that more than half a million such civilians had been killed. Under these circumstances, is it a matter for surprise that more and more Vietnamese are drawn to the ranks of the National Liberation Front? It needs only the sight of a red Viet Cong flag in a village or some, often unconfirmed, report that Viet Cong are in the village to draw down American firepower. The *New York Times* recently reported that most of the attacks by American planes on "suspected Viet Cong concentrations" are drawn down on the basis of reports from informers who usually do not live in the village in question, and on the basis of reports that are filtered through South Vietnamese army officers and then transmitted to Americans. Some of the most grievous mistakes have been reported in the press, but the mistakes occur all the time and the peasant villagers are in constant danger.

I was in a village with some twenty social workers the night that the Viet Cong attacked the Saigon airport with mortars. The mortars were not more than one kilometer from where we were, and we could hear the thump of their shells as they fired. A half hour after the attack had ceased, and long after the Viet Cong themselves had withdrawn, American planes came over on a reprisal raid. Their rockets and bombs ravaged the village. There were no Viet Cong there, and no Viet Cong were killed that night, but the village was almost totally destroyed and many of the villagers were badly wounded. At least one of the peasants was buried in the debris of his own house. If this were an isolated instance, it could be explained away as the kind of accident that happens in war; the fact is, that it is far more typical than it is isolated. Such events, and more tragic ones, occur every day, night and day, throughout our country. As the destruction and the terror intensify, so does the hatred of the villagers for the Americans, leaving the American soldier, who believed he had come to help, caught in a quicksand of hatred and frustration.

All experts on guerrilla warfare point out that such warfare cannot be successful without the support of the peasants. The fact that the National Liberation Front in Vietnam gets such support is explained to Americans in terms of the terrorism inflicted by the Viet Cong on the peasants: the peasants are too frightened to do anything but support the Viet Cong, according to the informants in America. This simply is not true. The fact is that the Front has the support of a considerable number of the peasants because it has been able to persuade them that this is in fact the struggle for national independence. The spirit of patriotism among the peasants is very high. They are not informed about world history or ideological struggles; what they see is a large force of white Westerners doing their best to kill their fellow countrymen, many of whom previously fought against the French. The peasants do not see the victims of the American military effort as dead Communists, but as dead patriots.

THE DILEMMA OF VIETNAMESE RELIGIOUS LEADERS

The majority of the people in the Front are not Communists. They are patriots, and to the extent that they are under the direction of the Communists, it is an unconscious acceptance of control, not allegiance to Communist ideology. I know it is a hard fact for Americans to face, but it is a fact that the more Vietnamese their troops succeed in killing, and the larger the force they introduce into Vietnam, the more surely they destroy the very thing they are trying to build. Not only does the Front itself gain in power and allegiance, but communism is increasingly identified by the peasants with patriotism and takes an increasingly influential role in the direction of the Front.

I do not mean that this is a simple situation. A huge portion of the Vietnamese peasant population is constantly torn between its almost instinctive support of the Front in its battle against the "imperialists" and the desire to follow the advice of their religious leaders, who warn them against supporting communism in their country. This is very important. The voice of patriotism impels them in the direction of support of the Front, while the voice of religion causes them to hesitate. This is true of all the important Vietnamese religions, including Christianity, with the exception of a relatively small group of those who emigrated from North Vietnam.

Americans should ponder the fact that the leaders of none of the major religions of Vietnam have ever declared themselves in violently anti-Communist terms, not because of any sympathy with communism, but because to do so, in the temper of Vietnam today, is to suggest that they are profiteering from the war through the acquisition of American dollars. In the past ten years anti-communism has become Vietnam's most profitable business. The most vocal of the "anti-Communists" may well be enriching themselves by their written or spoken contributions, but they are doing very little in fact against communism. On the contrary, by their support of the existing government and the American effort they succeed in perpetuating the very situation that strengthens communism. Thus the people with whom the government deals as the "good" anti-Communists are in fact those who cause much hatred of government and contribute more than anyone else to support of the NLF. If there is still a large portion of the peasants who have not actively joined in supporting the Front, and there is, it is because they still give allegiance to their religious leaders who caution them against doing so.

At the same time, it must be said that these religious leaders recognize that they cannot count on continuing to have the allegiance of the peasants simply by opposition to the Front. They must find other more constructive ways of combining patriotism and religion. They cannot keep the peasants with them unless they offer them another way by which they may express their patriotism. The peasants cannot help being intensely patriotic, and they know very well that no patriotism can be expressed through support of a government that is in fact a puppet, created and maintained by external power. The peasants see the present anti-American front as an extension of the anti-French front of the war of 1947-1954 and earlier, and this provides a legitimate outlet for their patriotic feelings. From time to time they hear of the evils of communism, but they do not in fact see these evils; what they see is the Viet Cong "fighting for national independence." The leaders of religions like the Hoa Hao, Cao Dai, Catholicism, and Buddhism can never advise their followers to support governments like those of Diem, Khanh, Huong, or Ky. (There were some government leaders during the past three years with whom many Vietnamese would have identified, such as Duong Van Minh and Phang Hoy Quat, but these were quickly overthrown with the consent and support of the Americans.) These governments, corrupted by the dependence on the United States in the absence of any real power of their own, can only continue the war in the unintelligent fashion imposed upon them by the Americans. They cannot attract the people, but are in fact constantly at war with them, liquidating and eliminating all of those genuine leaders who speak against their policies, and using the money and blood of the people mercilessly, creating more social injustice as they deepen the suffering from the war itself. These governments are looked upon by the people as an extension of the American government, and their policies as an extension of American policies. The budgets and policies alike of the Saigon government are prepared in Washington, not in the Gia Long Palace.

What Americans seem unable to see is that it is not the efforts of the Saigon government or their own military forces that have kept the full population from supporting the Front, but only the peasants' loyalty to their religious faiths in spite of everything that Saigon and Washington have done. And as the war is escalated by the introduction of more troops into Vietnam, so is the problem of these religious leaders escalated. If the leaders of Buddhism, who command the largest following in Vietnam, are not soon able to propose some alternative that recognizes the patriotism of the peasants, they will simply lose their influence. Even the Buddhist peasants will leave their leadership and turn directly to the Front. That is the crisis of this time: that the moderation of the religious leadership will soon be rejected by the peasants, and the leaders themselves accused of being puppets of the South Vietnamese government, unpatriotic, profiting from the war, and so on.

This cannot be emphasized too much: if the peasants still listen to religious leaders, it is because the latter have been very careful not to support the war policies, and indeed in some cases have raised the basic question of war and the voice of religious conscience. The Buddhist leaders especially have been eager to find a way in which they can express both the patriotism and the longing for peace of their people. That is why the Buddhist struggle has been going on. When they ask for a constituent assembly and an elected government, it is not for any desire for power for themselves, but for this reason. Their efforts have been suppressed by those who certify themselves as anti-Communist, and of course behind them stand the Americans, without whose help they could not manage. American policy-makers would like religious leaders to remain quiescent and keep hands off their war effort. Thus the Americans follow the old and fatal French policy of finding their allies only among the Catholics.

ABOUT LAND REFORM—AND VIET CONG TERROR

The essence of the war is this: The American effort could succeed if it could detach nationalism from communism, but the Americans cannot do this just as the French could not do it in their turn. What they do instead is to force these two elements closer together, and this is the reason why the Front constantly grows more powerful. By supporting elements with which the Vietnamese patriots do not identify, they let the whole power of nationalism slip from their hands and into the hands of the Communists. There are many fundamentally anti-Communist Vietnamese who know very well the Communist nature of the Front, but who still support it because it is the only alternative to the brutality and suppression of the government. The roots of the Front's strength in the will of the peasants have nothing to do with Marxism, but only with the peasant's basic hope to defend his nationalist yearnings and to oppose the oppressor.

Even the question of land reform, which is frequently referred to as a major reason for support of the Front, is not in fact that important an issue. I do not mean to suggest that land reform, and the absence of land reform, played no part in the war. The situation began during the war against the French, when many of the large landholders fled to the safety of the cities. In their absence, the Viet Minh took their landholdings and divided them among the peasants. When the war ended in 1954, and the Viet Minh by agreement moved to the North, the landlords returned to their holdings and in many cases re-established their claims.

Obviously this created considerable discontent among the peasants, and this was not alleviated by the partial measures of land reform subsequently taken by President Ngo Dinh Diem.

These measures, incorporated in Decree 57, passed on November 22, 1957, ruled that no landholder could retain more than one hundred hectares of land. The land thus taken from the landholders was to be sold to the peasants at very low rates and to be repaid over a long period. However, the results of this were not very helpful. By 1959, only 58,661 hectares had been so distributed, while tenant farmers still operated 1,469,197 hectares.

So there is an element of importance in the question of land reform as one of the factors in creating support for the Front, but it must not be overestimated. The total number of tenant farmers is not large compared with the total population, and the reversal of the pre-1954 land reform by itself could not possibly have created enough bitterness to result in the war.

Nor can terror explain the support that the Front receives. Certainly the Front uses terror and assassination, but it does not use them indiscriminately. The assassinations of village chiefs, about which people in the West hear so much, are a fact, but they are usually accompanied by a kind of trial procedure, in which the victim is condemned as an agent of the oppressive South Vietnamese government. The execution thus has an aura of legitimacy, and frequently is approved by the villagers who were under the control of the village chief in question. This is not to condone terror or assassination, or to ascribe to the Front humanistic motives. It is simply to look at the objective facts of the situation, and the objective facts are that indiscriminate terror, while sometimes used by the Viet Cong, is not the Front's usual practice. Nor can it be possibly described as being the source of the support that the Front has from the peasant population. Often, indeed, the victims of these executions were men who were hated by the villagers, and whose execution was in fact applauded by them. When this fact is added to the relatively small numbers involved—far fewer than some official figures have indicated, and hardly more than a thousand in all—and when this is compared with the tens of thousands who die indiscriminately as a result of American and South Vietnamese bombing and ground fighting, it is not difficult to understand from which side the peasants see the greatest danger.

STRATEGIC HAMLETS

Sporadically during the course of the war there have been expressions of interest in the idea of the "strategic hamlets." These were intended to draw people together in an area of some protection, and to make available to them such social services as would improve their lives and introduce the concept of co-operative efforts. On paper they look good. In practice, like every other promise of social improvement in the history of the South Vietnamese government, they turned out to be another device related to the military effort of that government. People were herded into the villages against their wills and the total concept of the village became a military concept. Peasants were forced to leave villages that had been the homes of their families for generations, and in leaving them to leave behind not only the graves of their ancestors but many relics and mementos, including family altars, which perished in the same flames that consumed the village. Thus they went to the new strategic hamlets already sorrowing and embittered, and hardly in a frame of mind to create a new kind of society. The hamlets were created to keep out the Viet Cong, so that the villagers could live in them and not be "intoxicated" by the Viet Cong, but the fact is that the Viet Cong themselves lived in many of the villages among their fellow Vietnamese. It was not uncommon to find in the conference room of the executive committee of a hamlet, on the morning that it met, the documents of the Viet Cong already distributed, and so the whole concept of the strategic hamlet was undermined and destroyed.

THE TOWNS AND THE REFUGEES: CORRUPTION AND MISERY

As in other countries, religion has its greatest hold outside the cities. The populations of the cities are more inclined to be "atheistic." The towns also include, however, the intellectual, humanistic, and religious leadership which, while not declaring itself "anti-Communist," is in fact the strongest non-Communist force in South Vietnam. Because they do not support the government, they find themselves frequently labeled "Communist" and, as in other countries, this is the surest way of making it impossible for them to operate effectively. Large numbers of them have been defamed, persecuted, and even exiled, and those who are left must live in constant danger, but they continue to do all that they can and have great prestige among the genuinely democratic non-Communist elements in the cities.

The cities are also the home of those who profit from anti-Communism and the war. They are comfortably housed and fed in relative safety, and desire no changes in their way of life. They are opposed to all demonstrations that might lead to such change, and live in what is for them the best of all possible worlds. Even their children escape the consequences of the war, since they are able to afford to buy them out of the draft. Since the war has become the national preoccupation of Vietnam, the various professions serving the war have become numerous and profitable. Literally hundreds of thousands of Vietnamese work at various services for the Americans, at their bases, on air fields, in their headquarter buildings, and in many other ways. Landlords are constantly seeking to evict their Vietnamese tenants so that they may rent their premises to Americans at prices that may be ten or twenty times as high as the Vietnamese are paying. An apartment that in 1960 rented for 1,500 piastres now can be rented to an American for 25,000 piastres. It is almost impossible for Vietnamese to find housing, since there are almost no Vietnamese who can afford such prices. Builders who compete with each other to construct new buildings for the use of the Americans have increased the cost of all building materials and services astronomically. This means that the ordinary Vietnamese is almost completely excluded from any possibility of buying these materials for himself. Similarly masons and other construction workmen are impossible for Vietnamese to secure since they are all attracted to the much higher paying jobs of serving the American occupation.

Taxi and pedicab drivers avoid Vietnamese customers for the far more profitable Americans. They do not charge according to the taximeter any longer. Americans, accustomed to costs in their own country, pay ten times as much as the normal rate for such rides, and in doing so of course also increase the pressure on the normal Vietnamese person. Some few taxi drivers refuse to accept this situation and continue to take Vietnamese, but then fill their cabs with customers going in roughly the same direction in order to compensate for it. In addition, taxi drivers frequently operate a profitable sideline in taking foreigners, especially American soldiers, to girls of friendly disposition who will compensate the driver in addition to what he receives from his passenger.

Bars, dance halls, and restaurants catering to foreigners thrive. The number of prostitutes increases daily and at a frightening rate; for many it is the only way in which they can support themselves and their families. Earning a living in Vietnam today is so difficult that the Vietnamese will consent to do anything, including selling their daughters and wives. In Da Nang a prostitute can earn enough to support four people—herself, the operator of the house, the pedicab driver, and the boy who brings the customers to her—while an ordinary worker cannot earn enough to support himself alone. Tradesmen and businessmen working with Americans earn large sums of money, while the majority of their fellow countrymen are going through a major economic crisis. Inflation that occurs from the hoarding of scarce goods for profit, the pouring in of American dollars, and the spending of great sums on nonproductive war enterprises—all this means that the Vietnamese without access to these American funds is in increasingly desperate plight.

As demand increases with more and more foreign troops coming in, the supply decreases through the destruction of gardens and farms by bombing and other military operations. Moreover, the war creates all kinds of obstacles in the way of the distribution of goods, including food, and this adds to the inflationary pressure on the economy. Similarly the American insistence that all aid and commerce must be with the United States and certain other approved nations prevents Vietnam from developing a viable economy of its own. In classic style, the government has now turned to printing additional currency in order to "improve" the situation, while in fact this increases the inflationary pressure on the economy.

Another large group in the cities are the peasants who fled from their ancestral homes, leaving their possessions and their farms behind them. They fled not only from the actual dangers of the war, but from the frustration of a situation in which crops may be grown only to be destroyed by one side or the other as a measure of war to keep the other side from getting them. Planes of the United States and South Vietnamese air forces drop napalm bombs on these crops so that they may be burned rather than fall into the hands of the Viet Cong.

Life for these people in the cities is very hard, and, without resources that they have not brought with them, they are forced into every conceivable means of keeping life intact. Each morning sees swarms of people on the dumps and trash heaps of the city, and especially on those adjoining American installations. The people organize into regular gangs in order to acquire the empty bottles and cans and sometimes full cans of food thrown out by the American forces. So the passer-by in the city is invited to buy the "very nutritious" American canned goods that have come off the dumps of the American troops. Most sought after, of course, are all kinds of jobs in connection with the American installations, since here again pay is higher than can be achieved anywhere else.

By early 1966 there were more than a million refugees living in camps in central Vietnam alone. Their life was tragic in the extreme. In principle they are allowed seven piastres a day for food, which is the equivalent of about four United States cents. That is enough in theory at least to buy about 60 grams of rice per day, but the minimum requirement for survival for an adult Vietnamese is between 600 and 700 grams of rice. Sixty grams provides hardly enough for a very thin soup for breakfast.

But, in addition, it is only in principle that they receive the seven piastres, since there are so many ways in which money is diverted into the pockets of those who profit from the war that frequently the refugees receive nothing. Hunger is so terrible that there are places where a young girl will sell her body for a piece of bread. Even the generosity of those who try to send food to help the victims of the war is frustrated by the corruption that has overtaken the whole country. Cans of cooking oil that are sent by donors in America or other countries reach the recipients emptied of the oil and filled with ordinary water. This is typical of what is happening to the refugees in Vietnam. In the desperation of war people forget every other value in the attempt to survive, and will do anything that advances their chances of survival.

In such circumstances priests and nuns cannot go on preaching morality; the war has destroyed not only human lives but all human values as well. It undermines all government structures and systems of society, destroys the very foundations of democracy, freedom, and all human systems of values. Its shame is not just the shame of the Vietnamese, but of the whole world. The whole family of mankind will share the guilt if they do not help to stop this war.

And in the cities also of course is the whole new suburban class who live off the war, in commercial, service, or functionary capacities, and whose new-found prosperity would disappear if the war were to end. They have thus achieved a vested interest in the continuation of the war, and are the ardent supporters of the government that carries it on. This group is one that is willing to carry on the war until the bitter end in order to "defeat Communism," but outside of this group everybody in Vietnam, including those in the cities, wants this destructive and race-exterminating war to end.

What Can Be Done?

NEUTRALISM OUTLAWED: THE FATE OF POETS, PETITIONERS, AND VISITING PACIFISTS

But how to stop the war? In Vietnam today no one has the legal right to speak for peace; indeed, those who do speak for peace put their lives in jeopardy. Speaking of these things, according to the Saigon government, is either "communism" or "neutralism," and, according to Saigon, "neutralism" is practically the same as "communism." Anyone who speaks for peace is in danger of suppression, exile, or imprisonment, and even a former Chief of State, Phan Khac Suu, when he speaks of peace, may not use the Vietnamese words *hoa binh,* whose meaning is unmistakable, but must use the words *thanh binh,* which is a more equivocal expression. If the Vietnamese people were free to express their will about the ending of the war, then the war itself, along with the presence of American troops, would lose its *raison d'être*. Officially the Americans are there at the invitation of the Vietnamese to save them from "communism"; if the Vietnamese people were free to say what they really want, this official reason would be exposed as the falsity that it is in the eyes of all the world. That is why the American and the South Vietnamese governments both try constantly to silence the voices of those who speak out for an end to the massacre and for means of achieving peace.

Early in 1965 La Boi publishing house published a book of my poems entitled *Let Us Raise Our Hands to Pray for the Appearance of the White Dove*. The poems were greeted warmly by the people and in less than a week 4,000 copies were sold. They spoke of hatred of the war and the desire to bring it to an end. But the book was not so popular with the official warring bodies. The Saigon government ordered it seized—fortunately after it had been sold out. Radio Peking, Radio Hanoi, and the Voice of the National Liberation Front denounced it.

The Saigon government said that the author was obviously a Communist. The other side declared, "His soul and body have obviously been entirely bought by the Pentagon and the White House." However the anti-war voice faithfully reflects the feelings of the peasants of Vietnam, and only a course of action that is consistent with their feelings provides any hope for getting out of the quicksand of this war.

On February 16, 1965, a courageous group of South Vietnamese intellectuals called on the South Vietnamese government and the National Liberation Front to cease fighting and to enter into negotiations immediately to avoid further destruction. It included university professors, doctors, lawyers, journalists, and other similar intellectual professions. They addressed their petition to both the South Vietnamese government and the National Liberation Front and in three days were able to secure more than 4,000 signatures. The text of their petition was as follows:

PETITION FOR THE STOPPING OF THE WAR AND THE REALIZATION OF PEACE, ADDRESSED TO THE GOVERNMENT OF THE REPUBLIC OF VIETNAM AND THE NATIONAL LIBERATION FRONT.

Inasmuch as the war in the past twenty years has brought so much destruction to the country, a war that is not created by the people of Vietnam; and

Inasmuch as the Vietnamese people are the direct victims of this fratricidal war; and

Inasmuch as this war can only increase and threaten to destroy the whole Vietnamese population and transform into a new world war on the homeland of the Vietnamese; and

Inasmuch as the Vietnamese people are willing to demand a cessation of the war and the people of the world also will to have peace,

We, the undersigned, belonging to all classes of people in Vietnam, have decided to ask the two belligerents, the government of the Republic of Vietnam and the National Liberation Front, confronting their responsibility in history toward the people of Vietnam, immediately to stop the war and make peace for the country.

Done in Saigon
February 16, 1965

The names of signers on the first page of this petition are those of Dr. Pham Van Huyen, Anam Tran Tuan Khai, a distinguished writer, and Dr. Nguyen Xuan Bai.

In a period of less than a week the movement was suppressed violently. Nearly one hundred intellectuals, leaders of the movement, were arrested. Many of them are still in prison. Three of these leaders—Dr. Pham Van Huyen, Dr. Cao Minh Chiem, and Professor Ton That Duong Ky—were deported to North Vietnam, crossing the Ben Hai Bridge at the 17th parallel.

Also at the beginning of 1965, a Buddhist monk named Thich Quang Lien, professor of the Faculty of Letters of Saigon University, grouped around him a number of intellectuals and students and created the Movement to Protect Peace and Happiness of the People. As soon as the movement had created an echo it was suppressed and Thich Quang Lien himself was "invited" to go to Thailand, where he has had to stay under the supervision of the South Vietnamese embassy.

The group of six Americans led by the Reverend A. J. Muste who went to Saigon in order to demonstrate against the war knew very well the attitude of mind existing there. They came to Vietnam to say to the Vietnamese people that there are Americans who understand the suffering that they are enduring at the hands of American policy, and who oppose that policy vigorously in their own country. The morning (April 24, 1966) that they organized a demonstration and press conference, the police and secret police of Saigon blocked the entrance to the Hotel Caravelle where they were staying. They finally did get permission to organize a press conference in the Town Hall under the supervision of the town authorities. They were met with tomatoes and eggs, and after that the demonstration had to be called off.

This counter-demonstration was organized by the police and secret police, and those who participated in it were their personal agents. On the same morning students and other Vietnamese who heard about it gathered around to applaud the demonstrators and to support them. But this crowd was dispersed so that the government-sponsored demonstration could proceed. The cars used by the secret police-supported group had their numbers carefully obscured by white papers pasted over the license plates, so that they might not be as easily identified as government cars. They were equipped with slogans protesting the presence of American pacifists and demanding their deportation. The signs of the American pacifists were torn and the Americans themselves were shoved into a car and taken to the airport for deportation. While they were waiting for a plane at the airport, the counter-demonstrators were transported to the airport to continue their demonstration. Although regulations for entering the Saigon airport are very strict, requiring the possession of a ticket marked with the date and the hour of the flight, these counter-demonstrators had no difficulty in entering the airport. If it had not been organized by the authorities, such a demonstration would have been completely impossible. Nevertheless, reporters and observers from abroad who witnessed the demonstration gathered from it that the Vietnamese as a whole are entirely for the war and want to continue it until the last Viet Cong is dead.

U.S. AIMS INCOMPREHENSIBLE TO VIETNAMESE

President Johnson has repeatedly said that the United States stays in Vietnam only in order to protect South Vietnam from the invasions from the North. The United States did not provoke the war, he says, and if at any time North Vietnam is willing to sit at the conference table to negotiate its end, the United States is willing. The people see that in order to force North Vietnam to the conference table, the United States has bombed North Vietnam, and has carried on that bombing since the end of 1964. And once again, the intention is not to attack or to provoke, but only to stop the transportation of weapons and troops to the South.

I do not know how the people of other countries think, but no Vietnamese peasant can understand these arguments. If the United States is determined to defeat the Viet Cong in order to protect South Vietnam, why should it offer to negotiate? To accept negotiation is not to pursue the very objective that the United States has asserted. The Vietnamese think that the talk of negotiations by the United States is only intended to quiet world opinion which is becoming increasingly opposed to its policies, and that the United States does not really want negotiations or peace. The Vietnamese remember several tricks that have been played on them in the past so far as ending the war and negotiations are concerned. For that reason, Hanoi could not believe in the sincerity of the United States during the thirty-seven–day bombing pause. Even though the Americans profess to be seeking negotiations, the fighting and bombing continued in South Vietnam, and the number of American troops landed during the bombing pause exceeded that of all North Vietnamese troops in South Vietnam at the time.

Even South Vietnamese people do not believe in the statements or sincerity of Washington; how then can the North Vietnamese be expected to believe them? After twenty years of war and broken promises, all Vietnamese people have become suspicious of the promises of the big powers, East as well as West. Unless the United States takes very dramatic actions to prove its will for peace, it cannot hope at all to win the faith and belief of the Vietnamese. What it has been doing so far is just the reverse. First the introduction of troops into South Vietnam was thought to be enough to stop the "aggression." Then it was necessary to bomb the Ho Chi Minh trail to stop the flow of men and ammunitions into South Vietnam from the North. When that did not work, and indeed the Viet Cong seemed to be growing stronger, the next solution was to bomb North Vietnam in order to bring that country to the conference table. North Vietnam did not come to the conference table, so the United States decided to bomb Haiphong and Hanoi.

Apparently that is still not the solution and the search for the roots of the trouble goes on. What will be next? The canals and dikes of North Vietnam, whose bombing will result in the deaths of tens of thousands more? Laos? Cambodia? The nuclear installations of the People's Republic of China? Peking? The escalation route of Washington is heading that way, and the survival of the human race itself is threatened. What Washington does not realize is that the root of the problem is not in the Ho Chi Minh trail, or

Hanoi, Haiphong or Peking, but in the heart of the Vietnamese peasant. The war in Vietnam has already lost its meaning, and the longer it goes on, the deeper the hatred and frustration in the heart of the Vietnamese.

The Vietnamese do not naturally look on the Americans as their enemies, but want them to be their friends. In the demonstration by the workers of Vietnam on May Day, 1966, the most prominent banner was one that said, "We want America to be our ally for peace, not for war." Each day that the possibility of peace is postponed, the prestige of Washington is diminished, not alone in Vietnam but everywhere in the world. Each day the war goes on the hatred increases in the heart of the Vietnamese and in the hearts of those of humanitarian instinct. The Americans are forcing even their friends into becoming their enemies. It is curious that the Americans, who calculate so carefully on the possibilities of military victory, do not realize that in the process they are incurring deep psychological and political defeat. The image of America will never again be the image of revolution, freedom, and democracy, but the image of violence and militarism.

"But if we withdraw, the Communists will take over. Would you like that?" American friends ask us. There are Vietnamese who are unable to answer this question. But not being able to answer it does not mean acceptance of a continuation of the present hopeless situation.

A THIRD POSSIBILITY?

An inability to answer that question means an unwillingness to accept the idea that there are only two alternatives: communism or the continuation of the war. The Vietnamese who cannot answer the American friend's problem do not want either. They seek instead a third possibility, and it is this that the non-Communists of South Vietnam are trying to develop.

Earlier I have said that the only way out is to find a way for the Vietnamese peasant to combine patriotism and peace, which is not the way of the National Liberation Front. For more than three thousand years the Vietnamese have resisted those who have tried to conquer them, and done so successfully, including even the troops of the terrible Genghis Khan. Patriotism is a deeply inbred force in them. But the corruption and violence of the South Vietnamese government have convinced them that it is not an adequate vehicle for their patriotism, only a puppet of a foreign power. The government of Mr. Ngo Dinh Diem at the beginning gave the impression that it would create a satisfactory government for Vietnam, but soon this hope was destroyed. The revolution of 1963 against Diem brought a new vitality to Vietnam, indicating that the people had the power to overturn a government that they disapproved of, but this vitality has been dissipated by the fact that the overwhelming power of the United States is directed against any faction in South Vietnam that expresses itself as having a will for peace. For today the Vietnamese people's patriotism is matched only by their desire for peace, and no government can possibly hope for their support that does not demonstrate its deep concern for peace.

Inattentive observers have complained that the struggle that has gone on against the Vietnamese government during '64, '65, and '66 has only been a means of hampering the war effort. But in fact this struggle has had throughout one deep and inarticulated objective: that is, the creation of a government that combines the genuine will of the people for independence with their profound aspiration for peace. The people of Vietnam have made their desires very clear. When Premier Ky announced the appointment of a "war cabinet," the people responded with demonstrations that said "we do not need a war cabinet; we need a cabinet for peace." The May Day demonstration in 1966 of the Workers' Federation declared this very clearly. The demonstration was suppressed and Mr. Le Van Thot, president of the federation, was imprisoned and continues in prison at this writing. The more the war is escalated in Vietnam, the more clearly it demonstrates how seriously mistaken the American policy is. What results is a spiral of mistakes, each one becoming an occasion for a new and greater one, all because each one produces new military attempts to answer it. Each bombardment has the result of pushing more people to the other side and giving more strength to the Front.

That is why the Vietnamese believe that the United States must change its policy and let them find their own solutions to their own problems. The non-Communist Vietnamese have to have a chance to bring into existence a force that will combine patriotism with peace, so they must be allowed to have an independent and pacifist government. America should respect such a government and help it to achieve the aspirations of the non-Communist Vietnamese. Those aspirations are to solve the problems of self-determination and of stopping the war. America should help such a government to prove its independence, not merely by declaration but by concrete actions. America should be willing to respect the decisions of such a government, including possible decisions to open talks with Hanoi and the National Liberation Front.

The non-Communist Vietnamese do not want to be the victims of negotiations between America and the Communists. They want to be represented in the negotiations themselves; that is why they have to be represented in the constituent assembly and an elected government. The present government does not represent them, but represents only a determination to go on with the war. That is why it is unable to enter into the negotiations that are necessary to end the war. A new government, free to develop its own foreign policy and to enter into negotiations independently, would have the support not only of the vast majority of non-Communist Vietnamese, but of those who now support the Front and even of many of those who are actually in the Front. This is because those who do support the Front are in most cases not expressing their support of the Front itself, but their unwillingness to support the dependent and unrepresentative South Vietnamese government. A government that is thus trusted by the people would then be able to undertake the kind of negotiations with Hanoi and the National Liberation Front that are necessary for peace, and later for discussions of reunification of the country.

These negotiations and conversations could be broken down into several steps, perhaps as follows:

1. The creation of a temporary interim government that would represent the religious and political groupings now existing in South Vietnam, particularly the religious groups since these are almost the only remaining centers of loyalty of the population. Such a government could work with a strengthened International Control Commission, or formally or informally with United Nations representatives, to establish a genuine constituent assembly and move toward really free elections at the earliest possible moment. Some people may ask what would be more democratic about such a government than the present one. Clearly it would be desirable if the next government could be chosen through free elections, but free elections can only be held if there is a functioning government committed to making them free; that is, guaranteeing freedom of opinion, freedom of the press, etc. A government which is rep-

resentative of the major religious groups would be so committed, where the present government is not.

2. Such an interim government would certainly ask the United States to stop all bombing attacks, both North and South, and to refrain from any offensive ground action, withdrawing instead to positions now held and assuming an attitude of self-defense until the elected government came into power and arranged for the long-term settlements. It would also appeal to the National Liberation Front and the North Vietnamese to accept a similar cease-fire arrangement.

3. Certainly the elected government would be the agency to negotiate with the United States for the withdrawal of its forces, probably during a period of from six months to a year, though it is to be hoped that the United States would immediately cease bringing in new forces and would withdraw one or two units in order to evidence its good faith and its determination to respect the decisions of the new South Vietnamese government.

4. I believe that such a new government would rapidly consolidate its hold on the people of South Vietnam. As it did so, it would then begin negotiations with the National Liberation Front, looking toward the creation of a coalition government for South Vietnam, and also toward the withdrawal of North Vietnamese troops from South Vietnam.

5. One of the urgent early tasks for the coalition government, once it was established, would be conversations with the North Vietnamese aimed at re-establishing normal relations of trade and diplomacy, while South Vietnam itself was stabilized and helped to recover from the terrible damage inflicted by the war. Such conversations would be the first beginning steps in the direction of the eventual, but perhaps far off, reunification that all Vietnamese want to see.

I do not suggest this as a complete and rigid blueprint for the way in which South Vietnam should go, but as an illustration of the kind of moves that are logical and could lead to peace.

Some Americans have told me that such a course would lead inevitably to a Communist take-over. It seems to me that this is an oversimplification. If the National Liberation Front were in fact 100 per cent Communist, then the fear would be justified, but it is not. Only a very small proportion of its membership, though admittedly including much of its top leadership, is Communist. The rest, as I have indicated earlier, are in the Front because it is the only possibility they have for expressing their patriotic and nationalist resentment of the presence of foreign troops. Given a different choice, there would be strong pressures within the Front to co-operate genuinely with a representative non-Communist force.

The only possible way of really weakening Communist influence in Vietnam is to take away from the Communists their claim to be the only defenders of patriotism. Then the course I have suggested would serve to liberate the non-Communist Vietnamese who now follow the Front from the Communist leadership and reduce the Communists to depending upon their own limited resources. Moreover, the key to this is the fact that both in and out of the Front people in Vietnam universally yearn for peace, and the surest way of winning their allegiance is to combine the longing for peace with their patriotic devotion to their own country and its need for independence. To provide them with a road to peace and independence that does not demand a still greater price in blood and in suffering is surely the way to win their sympathy and support. For her own prestige and self-interest, the United States would seem to have to accept such a solution, and the Vietnamese for their own survival must press her to do so. It is the only way that friendship can be maintained between Americans and the Vietnamese.

The same considerations of prestige and self-interest would compel the National Liberation Front also to accept this way. It cannot be overemphasized that the Vietnamese people, with twenty years of war behind them, will turn with trust and longing to a government that combines the concerns of peace and independence. If the National Liberation Front were actually to refuse to co-operate with such an elected government, and continue the war, it would lose all claim in the eyes of the peasants to any defense of either peace or patriotism. A refusal to participate in an effort that is clearly in the direction of peace combined with independence would brand the Front as the enemy of the people rather than their friends, and its own image would be tarnished and degraded hopelessly.

On the other hand, negotiations that might take place before such a representative government had been created would necessarily be between the United States and the Communist leadership of the National Liberation Front. In such negotiations the interests of the vast majority of non-Communist South Vietnamese would be poorly served, and those Vietnamese themselves would reject the results of such negotiations. Americans above all people, with a national existence founded on the idea of "no taxation without representation," should understand that the South Vietnamese must have their own duly representative government to engage in such negotiations.

PEACE ACTIVITIES OF RELIGIOUS
AND OTHER GROUPS IN VIETNAM

The responsibilities of the religious leadership in Vietnam have been both to raise their voices in the natural concerns of religious people for the suffering of their fellow citizens, and to find explicit active ways in which to implement those concerns and find a way to end the war. Raising their voices in their religious concerns about the war is clearly not enough; they must also develop clear, rational, and concrete steps in the direction of a realization of peace. The result has been the creation in Vietnam of a new force, not allied with either the National Liberation Front or with the United States policies, and in this new, militant, activist force the religious groups are represented.

Of course there are within the religious groups some who have not followed this path and who still depend upon foreign power and are reluctant to involve themselves in the struggle. Though they are a minority group, especially within the Catholic and Buddhist communities, they constitute a serious obstacle to peace because they are the ones who are supported and publicized by both Saigon and Washington. Contrary to a widespread impression in the West, co-operation between the Catholics and Buddhists is realizable except for a small minority in both groups who have in a sense been "bought" by the Washington policies. Both Buddhists and Catholics, along with the other religious groups, have a common base of great importance in their desire for peace and national independence, and actually are working together in these matters. A real communion and co-operation between the Buddhists and Catholics has already been realized in vital fashion among the younger leaders in both groups. These younger men share a broader and more open outlook than do many of their elders, who are still imprisoned in the bitter conflicts of the past. The younger intellectual Catholic leadership are finding ways of recovering from the earlier alienation of Catholicism from Vietnamese nationalism, and in this process have found the basis for genuine co-operation with the Buddhists. The Catholic policy of "presence," to which I have referred before, is not far from the Buddhist concept of "engagement." In a letter addressed to American intellectuals on July 15, 1965, a number of Catholic intellectuals in a group called the Hanh Trinh gave a good analysis of the situation in Vietnam and then concluded:

> The key to peace in Vietnam is the establishment of a non-Communist movement that can enter into dialogue with the National Liberation Front and be strong enough to compel the Front to abide by the decisions made in those negotiations.
> The basic condition of peace cannot be other than to establish a democratic force, not aligned with any power bloc, in which all basic liberties and freedoms are respected, in which Communists and non-Communists can co-operate to build a progressive society, according to the ideals of justice and freedom.[29]

This is the vision of all of those who have a conscience and an understanding of what is happening, and it is supported not only by the Catholics but also by the Buddhists. When eleven Catholic priests raised their collective voice for peace, the result was greater faith among the Buddhists in the commitment of the Catholics to peace. That appeal, made on New Year's Day in 1966, was the voice of the Catholic conscience in Vietnam. Addressed both to the United States and the South Vietnamese government, it read in part as follows:

> Let us not wait for some guarantee, as we did previously, before we sincerely decide to respect the life and liberty of the Vietnamese people of the North and the South and the fraternity that binds us together.
> Let us renounce the pretension that we will find negotiations and an end to hostilities through military victory; and let us renounce the ambition of implanting or of suppressing an ideology by subversions and bombardments, for these things can only lead to genocide and to a prolonging of the under-development and division of our country.
> Let the authorities of both parts of the country start a dialogue in the spirit of justice and loyalty, in order to achieve peace. This is the only way of creating the material and moral conditions which will guarantee all the Vietnamese people a free and democratic choice with regard to their future.
> Let the great powers respect the right of peoples to autonomy and to

[29] *Vietnam Vietnam*, No. 1, March, 1966, edited by Le Van Hao.

"auto-determination," and let them not contribute further to making the war in Vietnam more and more murderous, and thereby risking a global conflict.

Since under the present conditions of the war, the North and the South, as well as the great powers which sustain them, have in fact shown that they cannot put an end to the war by themselves or by any illusory anticipation of victory by one side and capitulation by the other, it emerges that almost the only way which might lead to the cessation of hostilities, to negotiations and to peace (which would at the very least prevent further bloodshed), is the recognition and the consideration and arbitration of the United Nations. We must sincerely appeal to and collaborate with this organization.

With all our heart we invite the men of good will of both the North and the South to surmount all forms of oppression in order to express courageously and freely the desire of the Vietnamese people for peace so that the responsible authorities can no longer ignore this desire or can no longer have an easy conscience when they fail to start negotiations for peace and when they fail to take every step and seize every occasion of realizing it.

On June 1, 1965, the La Boi publishing house operated by Buddhists published a book entitled *Dialogues,* which carried in French and English the letters of five Vietnamese writers addressed to the world's humanists, and calling upon them to raise their voices for peace in Vietnam. I was one of these writers, with a letter addressed to the Rev. Dr. Martin Luther King, Jr., the famous American Nobel Peace Prize winner.

I wrote, "The great world humanists cannot remain silent. You yourself cannot remain silent." Since then Dr. King has raised his voice several times about the war in Vietnam. During my recent visit to the United States to appeal for peace in Vietnam, I had the opportunity to meet with him in Chicago. We discussed the struggle for civil rights in the United States and the struggle for peace in Vietnam. In a joint press conference subsequently Dr. King declared that the Negroes struggling in the United States and the Buddhists struggling in Vietnam were bound by a common concern for peace and justice and a willingness to sacrifice themselves for this cause.[30]

In the same book Ho Huu Tuong, a famous Vietnamese scholar, wrote to Jean Paul Sartre; Tam Ich, a well-known literary critic,

[30] See *Chicago Tribune,* June 1, 1966.

wrote to André Malraux; Bui Giang, a poet, addressed René Char; and Pham Cong Thien, a well-known literary critic, addressed Henry Miller. The book has been reprinted twice in Paris by the Overseas Buddhist Association, and sections of it have been printed in magazines in the United States. In the meantime it is not permitted to circulate in Vietnam because of the repressive laws operative there against any statement for peace.

The official message of peace from Patriarch Thich Tinh Khiet, supreme leader of the Unified Buddhist Church in Vietnam, was read on December 12, 1965. This message has been widely studied by intellectuals and students in meetings called for "profound study," and which have resulted in the movement of prayer and action for peace. The present activist movement grew out of that message:

> The Vietnamese Buddhists earnestly and urgently appeal to the belligerents to find a rational basis to negotiate with each other in order to avoid the danger of destruction of this country and the people of Vietnam.

The student union of Van Hanh University in a major convention on March 20, 1966, resolved as follows:

> We appeal to all the people in groups in Vietnam to examine again the problem of the war in Vietnam. We appeal to the religious leaders of Vietnam, especially the Catholics and Buddhists, to remember their own great mission handed to them by history, to stand up and call for an immediate end of the massacre in Vietnam.[31]

Students at the University of Saigon at a meeting in the Faculty of Sciences on March 31, 1966, resolved as follows:

> —To work vigorously for the formation of an elected national government in order to solve the present situation in Vietnam.
> —Condemn the present government and its dependence on the United States in the matters of foreign policy.
> —Protest vigorously the war of extermination in Vietnam.[32]

On May 1, 1966, the Workers' Union issued a Declaration of Conscience in which the will to peace is very clear:

[31] From the *Bulletin Sinh Hoat,* Dai Hoc Van Hanh, Issue No. 6, April, 1966.
[32] From the *Bulletin Sinh Hoat,* Dai Hoc Van Hanh, Issue No. 6, April, 1966.

We protest vigorously all hidden decisions and actions that are designed to continue the war of extermination in Vietnam. We are
determined to continue the struggle for the right of self-determination
in Vietnam.[33]

Perhaps one thing that confuses Westerners is that while the
struggle is in fact a struggle for peace, its form must be a struggle for a constituent assembly and free elections. Usually the
leaders of the movements do not officially refer to peace. Their
reason is easy to understand: in Vietnam any reference to peace is
immediately interpreted as "neutralism" and that in turn is equated
with "communism." There is on the statute books of South Vietnam a decree promulgated on February 1, 1964, that outlaws both
neutralism and communism:

1. Outlaws any individual, party or organization that acts by whatever methods to realize directly or indirectly the goals of communism
or a pro-Communist neutralism.

2. There shall be considered as being pro-Communist neutralists,
those who have engaged in actions or propagation of the ideas of
neutralism. Such activities can be interpreted as threatening the
security of the state.

3. Those who have been found to commit the offenses in Paragraphs
(1) and (2) shall be tried according to Paragraphs (2) and (3) of
Provisions for Military Trial. Such offenders may be tried by military
court under emergency procedures without the privilege of cross
examination.

The government of South Vietnam has identified the word
"peace" with "neutralism," and, as shown above, "neutralism" in
turn with "communism." Anyone who knows how many people
have been arrested during the past thirteen years and exiled, imprisoned, or liquidated will understand why the struggle for peace
must go on in Vietnam under the euphemism of struggle for representative government.

In reality peace can be achieved only if the Vietnamese people
are represented in a government of democracy and freedom, and
democracy and freedom in government are preliminary conditions
that are necessary for the achievement of a peace that does not

[33] From the *Bulletin Sinh Hoat,* Dai Hoc Van Hanh, Issue No. 7, May,
1966.

hand the Vietnamese over to the Communists. Those who understand the situation will not condemn the religious leaders for
lacking a clear-cut program of development, or accuse them of
simply hampering the war effort.

IV. CONCLUSION

THE STRUGGLE FOR PEACE led by the non-Communist forces should be regarded as reflecting the hope and consciousness of the whole Vietnamese people. During my recent visits to the United States and Europe to appeal for the support of this movement I have met many people who are anxious to do something to help achieve peace in Vietnam. Some of them feel that they ought to back the United States effort in order to defeat the Front and so secure peace in Vietnam. Others think that they ought to back the Front in order to get the Americans out of Vietnam to secure peace. All of them are sincere, but they do not truly understand the situation. In reality the war in Vietnam cannot be ended by people who support either side. By doing so what they really do is to help the war continue and help destroy the Vietnamese people. The most effective way is not to support either of the two sides, but rather to support those Vietnamese people who seek a third way of achieving peace in the way that I have suggested.

The war in Vietnam began as a struggle of the Vietnamese people for independence and self-determination, but they failed to achieve that independence both in 1945 and 1954. Now in South Vietnam neither of the two belligerents can accurately claim to be representative of the people. On the one hand is the government of South Vietnam, which holds power only by the grace of American support and usually through military officers. On the other hand is the National Liberation Front, also not elected, though claiming to be the voice of the South Vietnamese people.

This is the surface impression of the war, but if one looks deeper one realizes that what has developed in Vietnam is an international, ideological war between the United States and the People's Republic of China. This is true even though China has no troops in Vietnam. These two great powers are demonstrating their fears of each other. Each accuses the other of abusing the Vietnam situation in order to extend its own power. Each side says that it must stop the other in Vietnam, since if the other is successful in Vietnam, it will use the same methods in order to extend its power over the rest of Southeast Asia.

There is no satisfactory conclusion to these conflicting positions, so the two go on with the struggle, meanwhile both claiming to be defending the freedom and self-determination of the Vietnamese people. In reality neither of them is defending freedom and independence in Vietnam, but Vietnam has become a victim of their struggle. The governments of North and South Vietnam are dependent on these two great powers, and for that reason in the ultimate analysis the war cannot end except by decision of these two powers.

If the war continues to escalate, the whole world's security will be threatened and a new world war will be in view. That is why other nations and groups, deeply concerned about peace, have become anxious about this situation and seek ways of ending it. The struggle of the people of Vietnam therefore has been to arouse the world consciousness to the dangers that exist in this war. They hope in this way to bring pressure to bear on China and especially on the United States in order to create the conditions that will make possible the ending of the war in Vietnam. It must be evident to everyone that this must include a changed attitude on the part of the United States toward China.

Such a change of attitude toward China and of policy in Vietnam must not be seen as a loss of prestige for the United States. On the contrary, the prestige of the United States has already been greatly damaged by its actions in Vietnam, and will be greatly enhanced by a change of attitude. The prestige of the United States is based upon its spiritual tradition of democracy and freedom, and grows only as the United States remains faithful to that tradition.

The Buddhists in Vietnam are willing to co-operate with the other religious groups—Cao Daiist, Hoa Haoist, and especially with the Catholics—in order to realize peace and reconstruction for Vietnam. Within both of these great religions there is occurring a revolution designed to make them more relevant to the problems of life. This is very encouraging and forecasts the development of a relationship that can be extremely important. Within the hearts of the Vietnamese people the determination to work for peace and a democratic society can serve to unite the various elements that have sometimes been divided, and lead them to an acceptance of each other based on this common interest. Through this kind of action they can overcome the obstacles and lay aside the ghosts of the past that have haunted them for so many centuries.

The revolution in Vietnam is going on at the same pace as the revolution within Catholicism and Buddhism. Buddhism's road to actualization involves it in great suffering both internally and from outside; the metamorphosis of Vietnam is also the metamorphosis of Buddhism in Vietnam. If Buddhism in the future can contribute something to the new ideology of the world, it will have been because of the sufferings that Buddhism is enduring these days.

Actualized Buddhism is not something really new, but has its roots deep in the past. The Vietnamese Buddhists, and especially the majority of the Northern Buddhists, understand that this actualization is necessary. Each country, each time, each place, has its own form of living conditions, and living religion must change and adapt to these so that it may be a part of the social milieu of its time. The forms of Buddhism must change so that the essence of Buddhism remains unchanged. This essence consists of the living principles that cannot bear any specific formulation. Being imprisoned in such forms would mean that the essence of Buddhism would be diluted and weakened, so that the discovery of new forms for Buddhism is in fact the way in which Buddhism itself may be perpetuated. The history of Buddhism has proved this to be so, and the experiences of Buddhism in Vietnam today are demonstrating the importance of this actualization. From the eleventh century on Vietnamese Buddhism has constructed for itself the spiritual nuances that have affected greatly the whole structure of Vietnamese society. The essential task of Buddhism during that time was to create a culture and a self-consciousness of its own that would resist the invasion, both cultural and military, of the forces of China. This is expressed clearly in the personalities of Buddhists and Zen leaders like Van Hanh, Ly Thuong Kiet, Tran Quoc Tang, Tran Thai Tong. The efforts of Buddhism in this present period are on the one hand to actualize itself within a new and changed cultural atmosphere, and on the other to protect and develop the spiritual heritage of Vietnam. This simply follows the line of Buddhist tradition. The spirit of openness and tolerance that characterizes Buddhism is a guarantee of its ability to adapt to new ideological situations as they exist in Vietnam in order to further the cause of peace.

APPENDIXES

Afterword

Our relationship in the Fellowship of Reconciliation with Thich Nhat Hanh began in the summer of 1965, when the Fellowship's Clergymen's Emergency Committee on Vietnam sent a team of a dozen American and two European religious leaders of various faiths to South Vietnam. The group, whose earlier and subsequent appeals to both sides to stop the war[1] have been widely reprinted in many countries, hoped to inform itself directly on the situation in Vietnam, but sought especially to meet its counterparts in the religious communities indigenous to that country. Foremost among these, of course, by history and present loyalties of the people, is Buddhism, and our group was both honored and greatly helped by conversations with such Buddhist leaders as Thich Tri Quang, Thich Tam Chau, and Thich Nhat Hanh.

The last named, especially, through his poems and essays, deepened our understanding and respect for the compassionate concern for man in the faith he represents. His letter to Dr. Martin Luther King, Jr., included in these appendixes, was a moving and persuasive explanation of the self-immolations that were so troubling to the Western mind. His poems, passionately antiwar, still reflect the compassionate man's understanding of the depths of good and evil in all of us, and created an immediate bond between his beliefs and those that, growing largely out of Christianity, had given birth to the Fellowship:

> Men cannot be our enemies—even men called "Viet Cong"!
> If we kill men, what brothers have we left?
> With whom shall we live then?[2]

In the months that followed, we hoped that one of these Buddhist leaders might visit the West, and especially the United States. But it is difficult for any prominent South Vietnamese, openly opposed to the war and critical of the existing government, to get permission to leave,

---

[1] "Mr. President, In the Name of God, Stop It!" and "We Have Seen the Anguish of Vietnam" (*New York Times,* April 4, 1965, and August 1, 1965, respectively).
[2] From "Condemnation."

and it was not until almost a year later, in May, 1966, that the opportunity presented itself. It came as an invitation from Professor George Kahin of Cornell University to lecture at that institution on "The Renaissance of Vietnamese Buddhism," an invitation arranged by Thich Nhat Hanh's friend from the days of his studies at Columbia University, Professor Robert Browne, of Fairleigh Dickinson University, who serves also as vice-president of the Inter-University Committee for Debate on Foreign Policy.

The Venerable Thich Nhat Hanh[3] is a scholar in the field of the philosophy of religion, and he felt at home on the Cornell lecture platform, but he had come to the United States for more than that. He was prepared to take great risks in order to try to tell the American people what Vietnam is like, what war is like, and above all what the Vietnamese peasants, with whom he has worked very intimately, think about what is happening to their country. Approached by Professor Browne, the Fellowship gladly agreed to help arrange a three-week tour for Thich Nhat Hanh to present this larger message.

The three weeks extended to almost three months, and the area to include most of Western Europe as the invitations multiplied. He traveled across the whole of the United States, appeared repeatedly on television and radio, was interviewed by newspaper and magazine representatives wherever he went. He met with prominent leaders in religious and other community organizations, with notables in the world of literature and art, with high officials in the United Nations, and with members of the Senate and House of Representatives and Secretary of Defense Robert McNamara.[4]

---

[3] The word "Thich" has been widely but erroneously interpreted as meaning "Venerable" or "Reverend." Its actual purpose is to replace, for the monks and nuns of Vietnamese Buddhism, the family names to which they were born, as the succeeding names replace their given names, and represents the family name of the Lord Buddha, Sakya (in Vietnamese, Thich-Ca; abbreviation, Thich), of whose spiritual "family" they have become a part. The appropriate title in Vietnamese, which is the equivalent of "Venerable" or "Reverend," is Dai Duc.

[4] One person he did not meet, to his great regret, was President Johnson. Although the President had been quoted only a day before Thich Nhat Hanh's visit to Washington as being "eager" to meet with anyone who could give him any new ideas about Vietnam, his Mr. Bill Moyers left word with a secretary that Mr. William Bundy, in the State Department, had been "designated" to meet the monk. Mr. Bundy, in turn, had designated a lesser official to fill this chore for him. Interestingly enough, the day when Thich Nhat Hanh did *not* see President Johnson was also a day when the President generously took time for one of his famous appearances as guide and commentator to the White House gardens for a group of passing tourists.

From the United States, in response to many pressing invitations, the slender Vietnamese monk went to Europe, under the continuing sponsorship of the Fellowship's International Committee of Conscience on Vietnam, whose earlier world appeal[5] he had signed. In Sweden, Denmark, Britain, France, Italy, Switzerland, Germany, the Netherlands, and Belgium he was even more widely reported on by all media. Members of foreign ministries and parliaments welcomed the opportunity to meet him, and in Rome he was able to make a personal appeal to His Holiness, Pope Paul VI.[6] At the end of an exhausting tour, he stopped in Paris to write this book, and to prepare to accept still more invitations to Australia, New Zealand, the Philippines, and Japan.

Thich Nhat Hanh came to the West repeatedly disclaiming the role of political expert. He had come, he said, to tell Americans especially about the terrible suffering and disillusionment of his people, and about the meaning of the Buddhist-led demonstrations against the Diem and Ky governments. Under his tutelage, the nature of the Buddhist intervention became slowly clearer to those who heard him. The monks who were daring to defy both General Nguyen Cao Ky and his United States protectors were neither dupes of the Communists nor ambitious would-be officeholders themselves. (Indeed, monks are forbidden to hold political office.) Rather, as he explains in this book, they had been driven to take the stand they had by their profound compassion for their suffering people, and by the fact that *there literally was no one else who could speak for the war-weary people and their longing for peace.* Far from being a departure from their religious faith, their actions were impelled by it. They spoke in the same anguish as did the ten thousand clergymen, priests, rabbis, and other religious leaders who pleaded with both sides to end the war: "We, who in various ways have assumed the terrible responsibility of articulating the human conscience, must speak or, literally, we should expect the very stones to cry out." [7]

This was Nhat Hanh's mission; yet as he moved about and the Western tendency to polarize and oversimplify complex situations became more and more evident, he was compelled to deal with specific political questions also. After a while, to simplify procedures, he put down on paper the principal questions of this sort, and his responses to them, and they, too, are included in the appendixes (pp. 101-106).

[5] "They Are Our Brothers Whom We Kill." See the *New York Times,* January 23, 1966.
[6] See pp. 108-109.
[7] "They Are Our Brothers Whom We Kill," *op. cit.*

Those of us in the Fellowship who had the opportunity to work, travel, and talk with Thich Nhat Hanh during these months, and to learn more of the Buddhist philosophy he expresses, have felt a growing kinship with him and his associates. We in the Fellowship find ourselves close to the Buddhists in that they have no longing for political power, nor any inclination to align themselves with one aspirant for political position against another. (Thich Nhat Hanh has said repeatedly that it is not General Ky whom they oppose, but the system he represents, and that another—even civilian, even Buddhist—premier following the same policy would be no improvement.) They are trying to see the tragedy of war in its full dimensions, not taking refuge in the age-old human tendency to see one side in a conflict as all good and the other all bad, but to recognize the way in which each degrades its own professions by the means to which it resorts, and to hold always in the forefront man's need for love, reflected in nonviolent and reconciling ways of dealing with human conflict. We were deeply moved and gratified when Thich Nhat Hanh elected to become a member of the Fellowship.

But this appeal to the truly human in man—this attitude that stands in defense of man against the dehumanization that purely political approaches produce—is itself an act of profound significance in the larger political process. Echoes of Thich Nhat Hanh's words in the West have been heard in Vietnam. With his friend Thich Tri Quang, he is continually excoriated by the Saigon radio and press as "Communist," while Radio Hanoi, smarting under the knowledge of the popularity of his appeals for peace among the people of Vietnam, labels him a "tool of the Pentagon."

For his courage, he has put his liberty, and even his life, in jeopardy. He longs to return to Vietnam, to the work he heads, as director of the School of Youth for Social Service, of training young volunteers to go into the villages in work of social reconstruction and improvement. Yet along with the pleas that his interpretation is needed in the West have come the repeated messages from his friends and associates in Vietnam, urging him not to come back for the time being, warning him that if he does arrest is not so likely a fate as assassination.

For he is the authentic voice of the wistful, almost unrecognized aspirations of all men, and most of those who listen to him set aside for a while their longing for the simplicities of full alignment with one combatant or the other to hear with a respect close to reverence one who asks for alignment with humankind itself. There is a voice in every age that speaks to us through the red mists of partisanship and anger, and above the realities of injustice and cruelty, reminding us of the common heritage that is our only hope. Thich Nhat Hanh's is such a voice.

> Here is my breast. Aim your gun at it, brother. Shoot!
> Destroy me if you will
> And build from my carrion whatever it is you are dreaming of.
> Who will be left to celebrate a victory made of blood and fire? [8]

Alfred Hassler, Executive Secretary
The Fellowship of Reconciliation,
The International Committee of
Conscience on Vietnam

October, 1966

Comments by Thich Nhat Hanh on Some Frequently Asked Questions About Vietnam

NOTE: *In his recent visit to the United States and Western Europe, the Vietnamese Buddhist monk Thich Nhat Hanh emphasized that his mission was a humanitarian one, designed to communicate to the West the deep desire of the Vietnamese people for peace, and to plead for help in securing peace. At press conferences and meetings, however, he was understandably besieged by questions of a more "political" nature, designed to clarify for his hearers the nature of the events going on in Vietnam and involving the Buddhists. The following is a summary of his responses to the most frequently asked of such questions.—A.H.*

1. It is a mistake to interpret the tension between the Ky government and the Buddhists as a struggle for power between two contending factions within a society. The Buddhist actions are the culmination of a growing frustration and despair on the part of the Vietnamese people growing out of more than twenty years of war to which they see no end. They represent the mobilization of non-Viet Cong nationalist forces against a government that is seen as simply an extension of American foreign policy. The immediate objective is a civilian, independent government; the motivation is the intense longing for peace; the test of the independence of the government is whether it is in fact free to make its own decisions on war and peace. The Buddhists do not seek political power for themselves, but a civilian government in which all religious groups will participate.

[8] "Our Green Garden."

2. Similarly, it is a mistake to balance the Buddhist-led anti-Ky, anti-U.S., anti-war agitation by a few counterdemonstrations identified as "Catholic." The anti-government demonstrations, though led by Buddhists, have included Vietnamese of all religious faiths. Because Buddhists are the most numerous, and because Buddhism is widely identified with nationalism in Vietnam, the Buddhists have become the focus of this expression of national feeling.

3. The Catholics are widely reported by the press to be anti-Buddhist and anti-Communist. I have been asked whether it is possible for Buddhists and Catholics to work together for peace and in building a stable government, and whether the Catholics' fear and hatred of communism are as great as is reported. There are several things to say about this.

First, the people in the village, whether Buddhist or Catholic, are concerned most that the war end. They suffer directly, and the possibility that their religion might be restricted under a Communist regime does not weigh very heavily against the immediate danger from bombs and battles.

In the cities, where most of the religious leadership is, the situation is more complex. Many of the Catholic leaders come from North Vietnam, and have a very strongly anti-Communist feeling. They have identified so completely with the United States that they are largely alienated from the people. But there are others, younger priests and laymen, who are also anti-Communist but who do not believe that communism can be combated effectively by military means. Like the younger Buddhists, they seek to deal with the real problem of Vietnam: the need for peace and social reconstruction, knowing that this is the real way to oppose communism.

4. Genuine Communists make up only a small portion of the National Liberation Front (Viet Cong), though they may dominate its leadership. The hold of the NLF on the peasants does not derive from their belief in communism, but from the Front's constant reiteration that it is fighting only the American imperialists and their South Vietnamese "lackeys." The 90 per cent of the population who are peasants speak only Vietnamese and have no understanding of differences between the French and American motivations. They see white Westerners (more Americans than they ever saw French) apparently occupying their country, controlling their politicians, bombing their villages, and killing their people. Even when the American claim to be defending them against aggression (by other Vietnamese) is heard, it

is much less convincing than the NLF's arguments. Every day that the war continues, therefore, is advantageous to the Front so far as winning the support of the peasants is concerned.

5. Thus the essential element of the war is not military but psychological. The United States, as the most powerful nation on earth, probably can win a military victory, but only at the cost of destroying the whole country and its people. In the process of winning such a victory it would lose any vestige of popular support.

If, on the other hand, the United States were to make it unmistakably clear that it is actually seeking peace and is committed to leaving when peace has been secured, the Viet Cong would lose much of its appeal. If the United States were to make strenuous and credible efforts to stop the war, and the Viet Cong were to try to continue it, the peasants, whose passionate desire is for the war to end, would turn against the Viet Cong.

6. The peasants do not support the war, and their interest in such things as "democracy" and "freedom" is slight as compared with their interest in surviving. Almost none of them support the Ky government, and only a minority actively support the Front. Those who do are not so much motivated by an attachment to communism, or by fear of terror tactics (though terror is used by both sides), as by the fact that they see the Front as the only alternative to the Ky-U.S. alliance. The intervention of the United States and a succession of governments-by-coup in Saigon have made it possible for the Front almost to monopolize the claim to nationalism.

7. Most Vietnamese are suspicious of American intentions. Many of them believe that the United States is interested in Vietnam principally as a base against China. They do not accept the argument that the war was caused by invasion from North Vietnam. They cite the U.S.-Diem violations of the Geneva Agreements and the subsequent repressions by the Diem regime as its true causes.

8. In the cities of South Vietnam many people do support the war and the Ky-U.S. alliance. They do so because they literally live off the war and the immense sums of money pouring into the country from the United States and from American troops. The same people are vociferously anti-Communist, while many genuine anti-Communists refuse to identify themselves as such because such a statement is widely taken to mean that its maker is "getting American dollars." Anticommunism has become a business in Vietnam.

9. The large majority of the South Vietnamese people are Buddhist. Without the handicap of U.S. military intervention and support of coups d'etat by military juntas, therefore, the Buddhists would have great political strength in dealing with the Viet Cong. Indeed, probably the same proportion of the Viet Cong as of the general population is Buddhist, and for most of them their first loyalty would be to Buddhism.

10. Buddhists do not accept the argument that there are no choices except that between victory and surrender. The combination of a cessation of bombing, North and South, and of all positive military action by the United States, with the creation of an independent, nonmilitary government in South Vietnam, offers another possibility.

Since it would be physically impossible to withdraw all U.S. forces immediately, it is politically unrealistic to suggest such a thing. However, a solid commitment to a complete withdrawal within a specified and limited time would be made credible by dramatic American moves in that direction. The widely heralded "pause" in the bombing of North Vietnam for thirty-seven days was not such a move, especially since it was accompanied by the arrival of still more U.S. troops. Even the South Vietnamese do not believe that the United States means to withdraw; how can we expect the North Vietnamese and the Front to believe it?

11. How can the United States withdraw with honor? What is honor? The honor of the American devotion to democracy and self-determination is widely known, but if that honor cannot be shown in Vietnam, then honor is not served. Stopping the bombing and shooting of Vietnamese will not harm honor. Honor has been greatly harmed by the failure of South Vietnam to honor the Geneva Agreements; there are valid reasons for North Vietnam and the Front to distrust the United States. It will take drastic, dramatic actions to overcome that distrust.

What would such "dramatic actions" be? Stopping the bombing, both North and South, would be one. Orders to the ground troops not to engage in any offensive action would be another. An unambiguous commitment to the Geneva Agreements, including a flat statement of withdrawal of troops and bases within a specified period (eight to ten months?), would be another.

12. With whom should negotiations be held to end the war? We share the feeling of those who say that the Front must be a party to any negotiations, since it is a party in the war. But so must a legiti-

mate, representative, independent government of South Vietnam. They are Vietnamese troubles to be negotiated; it is Vietnamese who should do the negotiating.

13. I am asked whether I do not think that the North Vietnamese should also withdraw their troops, and why I do not address an appeal to them.

Of course I believe that they should withdraw. I wish the war to stop, and through the widely published statement of the International Committee of Conscience on Vietnam in January, "They Are Our Brothers Whom We Kill," I have already appealed to the North Vietnamese and the National Liberation Front to meet their responsibilities for ending the war. There are three reasons why I have not emphasized that appeal on my present trip.

First, I have been speaking in the West and to the United States. I do not believe that my audiences generally have included persons with direct political influence in Hanoi.

Second, many Westerners try to relieve themselves of guilt for U.S. actions in Vietnam by maintaining that American troops are there only because of invasion from North Vietnam. That is not true, and my friends in the West should not be permitted to take refuge in this myth. Serious infiltration from the North did not begin until long after U.S. domination of South Vietnam was a fact, and the U.S.-supported South Vietnamese government had refused to carry out the agreed-upon elections. North Vietnamese troops are in South Vietnam, and I wish to see them out, but the principal reason for their presence there is the prior and growing American intervention.

Third, North Vietnam justifies the presence of its troops in South Vietnam by two things: the violation of the Geneva Agreements' provision for elections to unify the country, and the presence of the U.S. troops. North Vietnam and the National Liberation Front, lacking the supply facilities of the United States, are dependent on the help of the South Vietnamese peasants. If that help was removed, neither North Vietnam nor the National Liberation Front could continue to function effectively. Therefore the question of greatest importance is why the peasants help them, and under what circumstances they would withdraw that help. It is the answer to that question that I have tried to present, and I think it is clear. The most effective way of getting North Vietnamese troops to withdraw, and of disarming the National Liberation Front, is by persuading the South Vietnamese peasants that they have a better means of ending the war and securing independence. That can only be done by making possible an independent, civilian,

representative government for South Vietnam, free to make the ultimate decisions for peace; and by emphasizing United States willingness to end the war by stopping all bombing and offensive ground
action, and announcing a timetable for total withdrawal.

"In Search of the Enemy of Man"

*From a letter by Thich Nhat Hanh addressed to the Rev. Dr. Martin
Luther King, Jr., June 1, 1965.*

The self-burning of Vietnamese Buddhist monks in 1963 is some-
how difficult for the Western Christian conscience to understand. The
press spoke then of suicide, but in the essence, it is not. It is not even
a protest. What the monks said in the letters they left before burning
themselves aimed only at alarming, at moving the hearts of the oppressors, and at calling the attention of the world to the suffering endured then by the Vietnamese. To burn oneself by fire is to prove that
what one is saying is of the utmost importance. There is nothing more
painful than burning oneself. To say something while experiencing this
kind of pain is to say it with utmost courage, frankness, determination,
and sincerity. During the ceremony of ordination, as practiced in the
Mahayana tradition, the monk-candidate is required to burn one or
more small spots on his body in taking the vow to observe the 250
rules of a *bhikshu,* to live the life of a monk, to attain enlightenment,
and to devote his life to the salvation of all beings. One can, of course,
say these things while sitting in a comfortable armchair; but when the
words are uttered while kneeling before the community of *sangha* and
experiencing this kind of pain, they will express all the seriousness of
one's heart and mind, and carry much greater weight.

The Vietnamese monk, by burning himself, says with all his strength
and determination that he can endure the greatest of sufferings to protect his people. But why does he have to burn himself to death? The
difference between burning oneself and burning oneself to death is
only a difference in degree, not in nature. A man who burns himself
too much must die. The importance is not to take one's life, but to
burn. What he really aims at is the expression of his will and determination, not death. In the Buddhist belief, life is not confined to a
period of 60 or 80 or 100 years: life is eternal. Life is not confined
to this body: life is universal. To express will by burning oneself,
therefore, is not to commit an act of destruction but to perform an

act of construction, that is, to suffer and to die for the sake of one's people. This is not suicide. Suicide is an act of self-destruction, having as causes the following: (1) lack of courage to live and to cope with difficulties; (2) defeat by life and loss of all hope; (3) desire for nonexistence (*abhaya*).

This self-destruction is considered by Buddhism as one of the most serious crimes. The monk who burns himself has lost neither courage nor hope; nor does he desire nonexistence. On the contrary, he is very courageous and hopeful and aspires for something good in the future. He does not think that he is destroying himself; he believes in the good fruition of his act of self-sacrifice for the sake of others. Like the Buddha in one of his former lives—as told in a story of Jataka—who gave himself to a hungry lioness which was about to devour her own cubs, the monk believes he is practicing the doctrine of highest compassion by sacrificing himself in order to call the attention of, and to seek help from, the people of the world.

I believe with all my heart that the monks who burned themselves did not aim at the death of the oppressors but only at a change in their policy. Their enemies are not man. They are intolerance, fanaticism, dictatorship, cupidity, hatred, and discrimination which lie within the heart of man. I also believe with all my being that the struggle for equality and freedom you lead in Birmingham, Alabama, is not really aimed at the whites but only at intolerance, hatred, and discrimination. These are real enemies of man—not man himself. In our unfortunate fatherland we are trying to plead desperately: do not kill man, even in man's name. Please kill the real enemies of man which are present everywhere, in our very hearts and minds.

Now in the confrontation of the big powers occurring in our country, hundreds and perhaps thousands of Vietnamese peasants and children lose their lives every day, and our land is unmercifully and tragically torn by a war which is already twenty years old. I am sure that since you have been engaged in one of the hardest struggles for equality and human rights, you are among those who understand fully, and who share with all their heart, the indescribable suffering of the Vietnamese people. The world's greatest humanists would not remain silent. You yourself cannot remain silent. America is said to have a strong religious foundation and spiritual leaders would not allow American political and economic doctrines to be deprived of the spiritual element. You cannot be silent since you have already been in action and you are in action because, in you, God is in action, too—to use Karl Barth's expression. And Albert Schweitzer, with his stress on the reverence for life. And Paul Tillich with his courage to be, and thus, to love. And Niebuhr. And Mackay. And Fletcher. And Donald Harrington. All these religious humanists, and many more, are not going to favor the existence of a shame such as the one mankind has to endure in Vietnam. Recently a young Buddhist monk named Thich Giac Thanh burned himself [9] to call the attention of the world to the suffering endured by the Vietnamese, the suffering caused by this unnecessary war—and you know that war is never necessary. Another young Buddhist, a nun named Hue Thien, was about to sacrifice herself in the same way and with the same intent, but her will was not fulfilled because she did not have the time to strike a match before people saw and interfered. Nobody here wants the war. What is the war for, then? And whose is the war?

Yesterday in a class meeting, a student of mine prayed: "Lord Buddha, help us to be alert to realize that we are not vctims of each other. We are victims of our own ignorance and the ignorance of others. Help us to avoid engaging ourselves more in mutual slaughter because of the will of others to power and to predominance." In writing to you, as a Buddhist, I profess my faith in Love, in Communion, and in the World's Humanists, whose thoughts and attitude should be the guide for all humankind in finding who is the real enemy of Man.

Remarks to His Holiness, Pope Paul VI, July 16, 1966

On Wednesday, July 16, 1966, Thich Nhat Hanh was received by Pope Paul VI. The following is a summary of the remarks he made to His Holiness on that occasion.[10]

[9] April 20, 1965, in Saigon.

[10] On September 28, 1966, the *New York Times* reported that a papal peace delegation, headed by Archbishop Sergio Pignedoli, a close associate of Pope Paul's, had been dispatched to Vietnam. On October 19, 1966, the *National Catholic Reporter* carried a long report from the Vatican about Archbishop Pignedoli's trip, including the following:

"An audience that the Bonze Nhat Hanh had with Paul VI . . . this summer is believed to be the origin of Archbishop Pignedoli's trip. Nhat Hanh . . . invited Paul VI to Vietnam suggesting that Buddhist-Catholic collaboration would be more effective in promoting peace than efforts by the United States or Ky governments. The Archbishop in reporting back on the trip stressed the concord that he felt had been established between religious groups in Vietnam (and) about the widespread desire for collaboration in achieving peace."

In the Catholic community in Vietnam there are many young priests and laymen who are profoundly conscious of the unspeakable sufferings of our people; their longing for peace is intense, just as it is with the great majority of the Vietnamese people. Unfortunately, they have no voice, they have no support for raising their voice of moderation. The declaration of eleven Vietnamese priests of January 1, 1966, expressed faithfully and urgently the feelings not only of the majority of Catholics but also of the whole Vietnamese people. But this voice has been smothered by the military government of South Vietnam, and also by a group of Catholics who are so violently anti-Communist that they have identified completely with the American policy of escalation, and thereby for the most part separated themselves from the people.

With all my heart, I beg His Holiness to help us in this difficult moment. If His Holiness could speak to our Vietnamese Catholic brothers, advising them to co-operate with the other religious groups in Vietnam in order to put an end to this atrocious war, spiritual strength would then really have defeated the force of violence.

I think it would open up a new hope for a peaceful and honorable solution in Vietnam if His Holiness could consider a trip to Vietnam. His high presence, first in Hanoi and then in Saigon, might lead to a pause in the bombings. This pause is so necessary, in this time of blood and fire, to give the belligerents on our national soil time to think, and an occasion to change their policy.

Statement of the Venerable Thich Nhat Hanh, June 1, 1966, Washington, D.C.

Just this morning the U.S. Consulate in Hue was destroyed by angry Vietnamese youths. In the past four days five Vietnamese have immolated themselves by fire, some of them leaving behind messages explaining that their actions were in protest against U.S. policy in South Vietnam. During my short visit to your country I have been repeatedly asked why the Vietnamese people seem to have become so strongly anti-American.

I wish, first of all, to assure you that I am not anti-American. Indeed, it is precisely because I do have a great respect and admiration for America that I have undertaken this long voyage to your country, a voyage which entails great personal risk for me upon my return to South Vietnam. Yet I assume this risk willingly because I have faith that if the American public can begin to understand something of what the Vietnamese people feel about what is happening in our country, much of the unnecessary tragedy and misery being endured by both our peoples might be eliminated.

The demonstrations, the self-immolations, and the protests which we are witnessing in Vietnam are dramatic reflections of the frustrations which the Vietnamese people feel at being so effectively excluded from participation in the determination of their country's future. Eighty years of French domination over Vietnam were ended by a long and bloody struggle, waged and won by the Vietnamese people against overwhelming odds. During the twelve years since independence most Vietnamese have remained without a voice in the nation's destiny, and this at a time when the nation is being subjected to a destructive force far surpassing anything ever before seen in our country. If anti-Americanism seems to be emerging as a focus for some of the recent protests, it is because the Vietnamese people recognize that it is really only the awesome U.S. power which enables the Saigon governments to rule without a popular mandate and to follow policies contrary to the aspirations of the Vietnamese people. This is not the independence for which the Vietnamese people fought so valiantly.

The war in Vietnam today pits brother against brother, the Viet Cong against the supporters of the Saigon government. Both sides claim to represent the Vietnamese people, but in reality neither side does. The most effective Viet Cong propaganda says that the Saigon governments are mere puppets of the U.S., corrupt lackeys of the imperialists. Every escalation of the war, every new contingent of U.S. troops confirms these charges and wins new recruits to the Viet Cong, for the overwhelming majority of the Vietnamese people now thirst desperately for peace and oppose any further expansion of the war. They see clearly that the present policy of constant escalation only puts peace ever further into the future and merely guarantees an even greater destruction of Vietnamese society. There are now more than 300,000 Americans in my country, most of them knowing and caring little about our customs and practices and many of them involved in destroying Vietnamese people and property. This creates friction which generously feeds the anti-American propaganda, and the fact that the war kills far more innocent peasants than it does Viet Cong is a tragic reality of life in the Vietnamese countryside. Those who escape death by bombings must often abandon their destroyed villages and seek shelter in refugee camps where life is even more miserable than it was in the villages. In general, these people do not blame the Viet Cong for their plight. It is the men in the planes, who drop death and destruction from the skies, who appear to them to be their enemies. How can they see it otherwise?

The United States chooses to support those elements in Vietnam which appear to be most devoted to the U.S.'s wishes for Vietnam's future. But these elements have never been viewed by the Vietnamese people as their spokesmen. Diem was not, nor were Diem's successors. Thus, it has been the U.S.'s antipathy to popular government in South Vietnam, together with its hope for an ultimate military solution, which has not only contradicted the deepest aspirations of the Vietnamese people, but actually undermined the very objective for which we believe Americans to be fighting in Vietnam. To us, America's first objective is to have an anti-Communist, or at least a non-Communist, Vietnam, whereas the Vietnamese people's objective is to have peace. They dislike communism, but they dislike war even more, especially after twenty years of fighting and bitterness which has rotted the very fabric of Vietnamese life. Equally important, we now see clearly that continuance of the war is more likely to spread communism in Vietnam than to contain it. The new social class of military officers and *commerçants* which has been created as a direct result of the U.S. involvement, a class of sycophants who support the war for crass economic reasons, are not the people to whom Washington should listen if it sincerely wishes to hear the voice of South Vietnam. The Vietnamese people reject with scorn this corrupt and self-seeking class which cares neither for Vietnam nor for the great ideals of America, but thinks only of its own interests.

The opinion is often expressed that there is no alternative to the present U.S. policy in Vietnam, neither on the political nor the military side. The non-Communist alternatives to a military dictatorship are said to be too fragmented to offer a stable solution, and a cease-fire and U.S. withdrawal are considered unfeasible because it is feared that the Viet Cong will take over the country by terror. The Vietnamese people recognize both of these dangers, but they also recognize the utter futility of the present course and the catastrophic effects which it is having on our society. Furthermore, we do not agree that there is no alternative to a military dictatorship. The force of Vietnamese nationalism is such an alternative. Indeed, this is the sole force which can prevent the complete disintegration of South Vietnam and it is the force around which all Vietnamese can unite. But nationalism cannot attain its effective potential in the present Vietnamese political climate, where opposition to the government invites open persecution upon oneself and identification with it discredits one in the eyes of the people. More than a decade of this atmosphere has served to drive many of the Vietnamese nationalists into the National Liberation Front, and many others of them into an ominous silence. Last year an effort by a prominent group of nationalists to circulate a mild petition requesting peace negotiations between the South Vietnamese government and the NLF was so brutally attacked by the government that we are not likely to hear from them soon again, despite their having attained some 4,000 signatures in less than three days' time.

Today, the means for nationalist expression rests mainly with the Vietnamese Buddhists, who alone command sufficient popular support to spearhead a protest for popular government. This is not a new role for Vietnamese Buddhism, for in the eyes of the Vietnamese peasants, Buddhism and nationalism are inseparably entwined. The historic accident that made the popularization of Christianity in Vietnam coincident with France's subjection of Vietnam created this image. The repression of our faith by the French and by President Diem strengthened it. And today, when the Buddhist attempt to give expression to the long pent-up wishes of the submerged and ignored Vietnamese masses is met by the gunfire and tanks of the Vietnamese army, the Vietnamese people, Buddhist and non-Buddhist alike, clearly see whose action reflects our national heritage and whose action betrays this heritage. Thus, although the Vietnamese people may lose skirmishes because they have no foreign sources of support, the crude victories of the Saigon generals serve merely to weaken their credibility while confirming the Viet Cong's propaganda claim that the goverment cares nothing about the people. The Buddhist efforts are designed, not to weaken Vietnam's resistance, but to create a genuine will to resist.

Differences do exist among the Buddhists, the Catholics, and the other sects, but they would not be insurmountable if there were a climate in Vietnam that encouraged unity. But there are those who see a unified, popular, nationalist movement in Vietnam as a threat to themselves. Such persons help to sow disunity and then use the disunity which they create as a pretext for retaining power. No, we do not accept the evaluation that there is no alternative to the present type of government.

The second argument offered for continuing present U.S. policy is that a cease-fire and U.S. withdrawal would merely leave Vietnam to the Communists. This argument we must also reject. The Viet Cong grow stronger because of the mistakes made by Saigon, not because of their communist ideology or their terror. If South Vietnam could achieve a government which was clearly responsive to the basic aspirations of the Vietnamese people and which was truly independent, there would no longer be any basis for popular support for the rebels. Indeed, the rebels would have lost their reason to rebel, and if any guerrilla activity were to continue the Vietnamese people would have the will to resist it for they could identify it as being hostile to Vietnamese nationalism, contrary to the people's longing for peace and reconstruction, and therefore of foreign inspiration.

Since coming to the United States I have been asked repeatedly to outline concrete proposals for ending the strife in Vietnam. Although I am not a politician and cannot therefore suggest every detail of a satisfactory settlement, the general direction which such a solution must take is quite clear to me and to many of the Vietnamese people. It does not involve the U.S. in any negotiations with Hanoi, Peking, or the NLF. To the Vietnamese people such talks, if necessary, are the proper province of Vietnamese officials rather than of Washington.

My solution would be along the following lines.

1. A clear statement by the U.S. of its desire to help the Vietnamese people to have a government truly responsive to Vietnamese aspirations, and concrete U.S. actions to implement this statement, such as a refusal to support one group in preference to another.

2. A cessation of the bombing, north and south.

3. Limitation of all military operations by U.S. and South Vietnamese forces to defensive actions; in effect, a cease-fire if the Viet Cong respond in kind.

4. A convincing demonstration of the U.S. intention to withdraw its forces from Vietnam over a specified period of months, with withdrawal actually beginning to take place as a sign of sincerity.

5. A generous effort to help rebuild the country from the destruction which has been wreaked upon Vietnam, such aid to be completely free of ideological and political strings and therefore not viewed as an affront to Vietnamese independence.

Such a program if implemented with sufficient vigor to convince the now understandably skeptical Vietnamese people of its sincerity offers the best hope for uniting them in a constructive effort and for restoring stability to South Vietnam.

The plan is not perfect, for the question remains of how the U.S. can be sure that the South Vietnamese government and the Viet Cong would co-operate in such a venture. Insofar as the South Vietnamese government is concerned, the past statements of Premier Ky have clearly indicated his unwillingness to seek a peaceful end to the war. In fact, it has been the contradiction between the aggressive words of Saigon and the peaceful statements of Washington which has so discredited the so-called U.S. peace offensive of last winter. The withdrawal of the U.S. support for Ky may thus be a necessary precondition for implementation of such a plan.

It is obviously not possible to predict the response of the Viet Cong to such a program but the installation of a popular government in South Vietnam, plus a cease-fire and the beginnings of an American withdrawal, would so undercut the Viet Cong's position that it is likely to have no alternative but to co-operate.

Finally, if some may question why I ask the U.S. to take the first step, it is because the U.S. is militarily the strongest nation in the world. No one can accuse it of cowardice if it chooses to seek peace. To be a genuine leader requires moral strength as well as big guns. America's history suggests that she has the potential to provide the world this leadership.

Statement of the Venerable Thich Nhat Hanh on the Vietnam National Day, November 1, 1966

This is a statement directly addressed to my brothers in the National Liberation Front. This comes after my appeal to religious leaders, humanists, and intellectuals of all countries, asking them to denounce all intentions of the United States and the Communist bloc to extend the war in Vietnam.

Vietnam National Day has the symbolic value for the co-operation of all Vietnamese, whether they are in the National Liberation Front or not, in the struggle against dictatorship, in the spirit of national revolution, in the will of self-determination.

I would like to take the opportunity to appeal for the co-operation of all patriotic Vietnamese, which is absolutely necessary in this struggle for peace and national independence.

No Vietnamese will refuse this struggle for peace and independence. That is why there is no reason for brothers to kill each other.

There are Vietnamese who have been supporting the National Liberation Front because they are convinced that the Front is fighting for national independence. There are many other Vietnamese who do not support the Front because they suspect that the Front may be driving the nation to Communism. This worry is increasing every day, because, as the war goes on, as the U.S. increases its army and weapons, the Front has to lean more and more on the Communist bloc to be able to cope with the U.S., and thus become more and more an instrument of the Communist bloc.

I oppose the U.S. because of its violation of Vietnamese sovereignty, and its direct engaging in the killing of Vietnamese. I also oppose the Communist intention to make use of the nationalistic feeling of the Vietnamese people to serve their ideology. But I respect all patriotic Vietnamese who are sincerely struggling for peace, independence and self-determination above all else.

I am calling for my brothers in the National Liberation Front to recognize the presence of patriotic, non-Front blocs of citizens who are anti-Communist, but who are also opposing U.S. policy, and seek to establish as soon as possible dialogue, co-operation and unity, beyond ideology, for the common purpose of Vietnamese self-determination. Thus could the Vietnamese people become capable of preventing the manipulation of the Front by the Communist bloc, and effectively stop U.S. interference in Vietnam affairs which violates the principle of self-determination.

That dialogue and co-operation between different groups in South Vietnam will certainly result in the establishment and guarantee of genuine neutrality in South Vietnam, eliminating all influences from the American and Communist blocs and realizing the peace that the people of Vietnam so desire.

We ask our brothers to act in order to avoid in time the threat of total destruction brought about by the U.S. and the threat of Communism inflicted on us by the Communist bloc. Only the co-operation between non-Communist groups and the Front can lead Vietnam out of this dangerous situation.

I pray for love to be seen among brothers and for the realization by all Vietnamese that their future and survival does not depend on the U.S., the Soviet Union, or China, but on the co-operation of the Vietnamese themselves.